# AUTO/ETHNOGRAPHIES

## Borgo Press Books by Michael Hemmingson

*The Rose of Heaven*
*In the Background Is a Walled City*
*How to Have an Affair and Other Instructions*
*Barry N. Malzberg: Beyond Science Fiction*
*The Dirty Realism Duo: Charles Bukowski and Raymond Carver*
    *on the Aesthetics of the Ugly*
*Sexy Strumpets and Troublesome Trollops*
*Vivacious Vixens and Sultry Sluts*
*The Yacht People*
*Seven Women*
*Hold Me, Please, and Say This Is Love*
*Give Me the Gun, She Says*
*Auto/Ethnographies*
*The Stripper*

## FOR OTHER PRESSES

*The Naughty Yard* (Permeable Press, 1994)
*Crack Hotel* (Permeable Press, 1995)
*The Mammoth Book of Short Erotic Novels* (Carroll & Graf, 2000)
*The Mammoth Book of Legal Thrillers* (Carroll & Graf, 2001)
*Wild Turkey* (Forge, 2001)
*The Comfort of Women* (Blue Moon, 2002)
*My Fling with Betty Page* (Eraserhead Press, 2003)
*Drama* (Blue Moon, 2003)
*The Rooms* (Blue Moon, 2003)
*House of Dreams Trilogy* (Avalon, 2004)
*Expelled from Eden: A William T. Vollmann Reader* (Thunder's Mouth
    Press, 2004)
*Zona Norte: Sex Workers in Tijuana and San Diego – An Au-
    to/ethnography of Desire and Addiction* (Cambridge Scholars, 2008).
*William T. Vollmann: Freedom, Redemption, and Prostitution* (McFarland,
    2009)
*Gordon Lish and His Influence on 20$^{th}$ Century Literature: The Life and
    Times of Captain Fiction* (Routledge, 2009).
*The Reflexive Gaze of Critifiction: Studies in Contemporary American
    Metatext* (Guide Dog Books, 2009).

# AUTO/ETHNOGRAPHIES

## SEX AND DEATH AND SYMBOLIC INTERACTION IN THE EIGHTH MOMENT OF QUALITATIVE INQUIRY

### SEVEN ESSAYS ON THE SELF-ETHNOGRAPHY OF THE SELF

by

## MICHAEL HEMMINGSON

## THE BORGO PRESS

*An Imprint of Wildside Press LLC*

**MMIX**

For Liv and Pabst

The aspects of things that are most important for us are hidden because of their simplicity and familiarity.

—Wittgenstein

Words too close to life *expose*.
—Trinh T. Minh-ha

# CONTENTS

# ANTHROPOLOGY OF THE MEMORIAL

## AUTO/ETHNOGRAPHIC NOTES ON AMERICAN RITUALS ASSOCIATED WITH DEATH

This essay is performance-based ethnography (Denzin, 2003) as well as auto/ethnography (Reed-Donahay, 1997; Ellis, 2004)—it is a meditation on the death of a friend and the ritual of collaborative, public grieving known as the memorial, as practiced in one sector of contemporary American society. I use narrative to examine this sociological event (Maines, 1993). The attendees at the memorial and I engage in the cultural performance of remembering well of those who have passed on. This event is life theater, or reality theater (Saldana, 2004), in which the performance-based aspects of a memorial can be categorized.

My method here is systematic sociological introspection , as defined by Ellis (1991a) through the technique of "first person sociology" (Kolker, 1996), now generally known as auto/ethnography in qualitative research.[1] Through sociological introspection (Ellis, 1991a), "ethnographers can make use of any at hand situations they are involved with as a topic of research" and also "makes the interior world, or subjectivity of the researcher in question, the object of study" (Roani,1997, p. 418). Ronai is an auto/ethnographer, following the notion that auto/ethnography "is self-awareness about and reporting of one's own experiences and introspections as primary data source" (Patton, 2002, p. 26). Ethnography is the writing of culture, so must be the act of auto/ethnography: "If one could do participant observation with others, why not with the self as subject?" (Ellis, 1995, p. 422). Van Maanen (1988, p.106) refers to auto/ethnography as a "wet term signaling the cultural study of one's own people" when discussing the work of Hayano (1979)[2] and categorizes the method as both confessional and impressionist tales (p. 102). For this account, I would classify it within Van Maanen's (1988, p. 73-79) framework of a "confessional tale" where

> authors normalize their presence coming on the scene, in the scene, and leaving the scene. Adequate ethnographic practice in the confessional requires fieldworkers to tidy up their roles and tell how they think they were received and viewed by others in the field.

I hesitate to claim I am "in the field" when attending the memorial of a dead friend, but I realize that the qualitative researcher—the auto/ethnographer—is *always in the field*, because his/her lived experience is a never-ending research project that examines, much like ethnomethodology (Garfinkel, 1969), every day social structures, the intersection of (auto)biography and history (Mills, 1959) and cultural changes that are moving in the sphere of the self (Cary, 1999). This auto/ethnographic account is an observation of a small group of people, a tribe if you will, in southern California, experiencing and collaborating in the same event: the ritualistic act of remembering the good things about the dead. I am a member of that tribe.

## LITERATURE

Many auto/ethnographic accounts deal with the death of a loved one and how the reflexive "I" deals with that loss (Ellis, 1993, 1995, 1998; Lee, 2006, 2007; Berg & Trujillo, 2008), comes to terms with memory and secrets (Ronai, 1996; Poulos, 2008), and finds the strength to "go on" (Berg & Trujillo, 2008). This writing of the *mystory* text (Denzin, 1988) and use of reflection is a healing process for the emotionally injured ethnographic "I" (Ellis, 2004). Before categorizing this form of writing as auto/ethnography, Ellis (1991b) referred to it as emotional sociology, that Kolker (1996) later dubbed "first person sociology" when writing about a personal event that had larger social implications. It should be noted, however, that while Ellis (1991a, 1991b) was developing what was then a radical theory, she was admonished by peer reviewers that the self, as a sample of one, raised questions of validity (Ellis, 1995). Today, auto/ethnography is an accepted method of qualitative research in anthropology, sociology, communications, nursing, health, curriculum, sports, leisure, travel, and postcolonial studies—it crosses from the social sciences to the humanities and often blurs the line between the two, what is sometimes referred to as a "messy text" (Speedy, 2008).

Anthropologists have always been fascinated with the social rituals of the tribes on remote islands and the villages of isolated societies, observing similarities and differences in other cultures. Haland (2008), for example, collects essays that reveal how similar the rituals of everyday life, pain, and death are for women across marginalized Europe. Behar (1991), however, "laments that anthropologists seek rootedness and meaning in the stories of exotic 'others' while distancing themselves from their own roots" (cited by Kolker,

11

1996, p. 134). Behar (1996) also calls for anthropology that breaks the heart of the ethnographer and the reader; death and loss seems to effectively do that, and many broken hearts will be found at memorials, as I discovered, including my own.

Rituals are collective performances (Conquergood, 1985) where individuals share the same experience (Kapferer, 1986). Anthropologists are always interested in observing, or participant-observing, the rituals of the other, from Balinese cockfighting (Geertz, 1973), youth courtship and sexual interaction (Meade, 1928), a rite of passage in the hunting of animals (Rosaldo, 1986), groups behaving during a carnival (Stewart, 1986) and the act of communal, performative bathing (Durham, 2005). There are various facets of collectively dealing with, and communicating about, death in contemporary American society via ritualistic gatherings: the funeral, the memorial, and the wake. The funeral is often religious in nature, where prayers are uttered and hymns sung, and the dead body is buried or ashes entombed. The memorial is reflective, where the dead person's family, friends, and associates (maybe enemies) come together to say prayers, recall experiences with the deceased, and generally speak well of the person who is gone. The wake often has a party-like atmosphere, or *is* a party, where the living celebrate the life of the dead.

## DEATH OF A FRIEND

Giggles[3] called and said, "Hey," and said our mutual friend Cindy was dead, had died several days ago; there was going to be a memorial on Friday. "You should go," she said; "I want you to."

"Dead. What the hell happened?"

"Brain aneurysm," Giggles said. "I found her. Went over there for a bar-be-que and there she was. I—I found her."

"I'm sorry."

"Will you go?" she asked.

"Not sure," I said. "This feels weird," I said.

"Yeah, it does," she said, "it does."

Silence.

"It would be good to see you there."

"Wait," I said, "*you* found her you said?"

"Yeah."

"On the..."

"She was in bed."

"Not the floor."

"She died in her sleep. They said she didn't suffer."

"How..."

"She had been complaining of headaches," she said. "She went to Kaiser and they wanted to prescribe her this medicine but it was really expensive, she couldn't afford it, so she decided not to. If this were Canada," Giggles said, "she'd still be alive, you think?"

I didn't know what to think about anything; at that moment, I felt like I knew nothing and knew that any minute, any second, I too would have a brain aneurysm and keel over.

You never know...

*"Have you ever felt a shadow creeping up into your mind, over your heart, through your consciousness?"* asks Poulos (2008, p.48).

"You guys were close," Giggles said, "for a while."

"Two years ago," I said.

"She asked about you now and then."

"Did she?"

"Yeah."

"What did you say?"

"Oh, I told her you were still writing books and that you were shooting a movie. She was glad for you," Giggles said. "She cared about you," Giggles said.

You never know...

"So you should go," Giggles said.

## THE MEMORIAL

There was no way out of it. I don't care to attend events for the dead. I can deal with the dead, I don't like being around the living that are grieving for said dead. "Do not feel sad for Cindy," one of her friends declared at the memorial, "because she is in a better place, where there is only love and no more pain. Feel sad for your loss, all our loss. Grieve for the hole that is now in all our lives."

The memorial was held at non-denominational church in a neighborhood I had lived in ten years ago. It was by a cheap motel that I and a married woman I was having an affair with once used as a rendezvous point. Memories I didn't want to recall filled my mind. I didn't want to revisit memories of Cindy either; surrounded by her friends and family, and the mutual people we knew, would inevitably bring up questions of, "How did you know...?" and, "Remember when..." Not that the memories were bad (at least from my perspective), they were simply—futile. Sad, perhaps. Giggles said we were "close." We had sex now and then, we spent some time together, but we both knew it meant nothing; we were just keeping loneliness away for a few hours by connecting physically, without much emotion attached.

I suspected there would be drinking in honor of Cindy—Cinder—because she loved to drink. Champagne was her "thing." She and I could go through three bottles in three hours. But she drank until she passed out; she was an alcoholic, a chain smoker, never married, no children. She had a long-term ex-boyfriend who was constantly in and out of prison and living on the street, selling and using speed. She was afraid he'd find out where she lived and want to move in with her. She was afraid she'd succumb to his demands, as she did for ten years.

She lived in a large house in southern California neighborhood known as Little Italy, an arts and restaurant community near the airport. She was roommates with six people, two whom were my friends. I had heard of this house before, many actors had once lived there. It was legendary in the local arts community. There was always a party on Saturday nights, a bar-be-que on Sunday. This is how I met her; this is how I started staying over some nights after a party. It was casual. She wasn't looking for anyone and I was suffering in a relationship (if you can call it that) with a woman I loved very much and who did nothing but hurt me, lie to me, and never keep her word and promises (and was severely bi-polar); I kept going back, though, the same way Cindy would return to the criminal ex-boyfriend...need, hope, addiction, co-dependency, masochism, who knows—what a pair, Cinder and I.

Cindy knew I would only go to the parties, seek her out, be nice to her, touch her, when things were bad with the woman I loved who in turn loved to hurt me; she knew but never talked about it, mentioned it; I didn't think she cared. Her friends, however, accused me of using her. This was one of the reasons I was uncomfortable about showing up to this memorial—would these friends attack me with vitriolic words again, speechifying about what a bad person I was for "utilizing" her for sex? I wanted to say, "She made use of me too, we exploited each other; it was symbiotic that way," but it was none of their business, really. None at all.

Her friends were cordial, however, and smiled when I walked into the space of mourning. They were hurting, they were lamenting, they said it was nice of me to be present and pay respects.

I felt forgiven and it was a warm, if not relieved sentiment. I didn't know why. I didn't feel I ever did anything wrong. I never hurt her, she never hurt me. I simply did not fulfill the biased expectations of those who cared for her. Let's say that their reality did not meet eye to eye with my reality (see Gubrian, 1988).

Still, I *was* absolved now—perhaps for everything in my life in that single moment, a fleeting period of general love and kindness when all former trespasses and blunders are elapsed and exonerated, like the final scene in the movie *Solaris*, where the characters are able to return to a blissful moment in their lives and exist in that frozen time where they only know love and peace, and all sins are washed away.

The church was full, every space taken in the pews—so many friends, so many co-workers, so many people with very kind and beautiful things to say about the dead.

I wondered, if I were to die suddenly, would I have such a memorial—would I have friends who would arrange it, attend it, and say good sentences about me?

Strangers introduced themselves, shook my hand, asked me how I knew Cinder. One was a lawyer; she looked familiar and I wondered if I had met her before—short blonde hair, big blue eyes, where and when had we crossed paths?

She sat next to me, she touched my face, she took my hand when the group bowed their heads down for prayer. We didn't need to know each other for this contact; we were connected by the dead. She needed someone to touch, a hand to hold, and I was agreeable to provide.

"How did you know her?" this woman whispered to me.

"Through friends," I said. "Giggles and Marty..."

"You were one of the roommates?" she inquired.

"No," I responded.

"I *know* who you are," she said. She squeezed my hand. "She told me about you," she said.

I said, "...why did you ask?"

"Curious about what you'd say; what she meant to you."

"...friends," I said.

What did she want me to admit?

"Were. And," she said.

And I said, "And things change."

## GAZING ON THE PAST

There was no reason that I could determine for the distance between us the past two years. There was no possibility of a serious relationship. Cindy was ten years older than me, and I was okay with that; she drank too much, she was always sad, even with that "infectious smile and laugh" many people commented on during the memorial. No one said anything about her being broken, heartbroken by life, by missed opportunities, unrealized dreams; about spending a decade with a man who could not read or write and refused to work and wound up on the street, and then prison; broken by an endless stream of dead-end, low-paying jobs and crappy cars al-

17

ways failing and dying; broken by waking up with a strange man in bed and not remembering what happened (I was one of those bodies).

It was her desolation that drew me to her two years ago.

Because I was sad, too, I wanted to connect with someone experiencing the same.

Because I was broken, too, I thought that wounded people could help each other heal.

She couldn't help me and I couldn't help her, but we did have some moments when we laughed together, were tender toward one another. We could just lounge around, relax, watch TV, do nothing, think about nothing; zilch, nada. Just "be."

I was drawn to her spirituality—she was interested in the Tarot, psychic readings, past life regression, angels and aliens and lost civilizations of antiquity. She took me to reiki healings, introduced me to friends who claimed to be psychic readers and/or alien contactees. I needed the distraction back then.

Return to the Memorial

"The three of us knew each other in a past life, in a distant time and another world," said the stranger holding my hand. "Do you remember?"

I lied: "Of course," knowing she was testing me again.

I tried to contact Cindy's spirit before going to the memorial, to hear what she had to say. There was no connection. I would never hear her voice again.

Wait. I *could.* I called her cell phone. It was still active, the voice mail was still on.

"Goodbye, my friend," is the message I left. "Say hello to my son for me."

I imagined what I would have done, how I would have reacted, had she answered the phone. "What do you mean I'm *dead*? Are you *crazy*?" she would have said, and: "Whatever—talk to the hand, guy!"

Songs, prayers, tears. People with children—infants and teens. Photographs, flowers, and two cases of champagne. She would have approved of the booze.

I was scared. I was afraid. If I died tonight in my sleep, I thought, if my brain burst a blood vessel like Cindy's did, who would find my body? Who would notice I wasn't around? Who would arrange for a church, flowers, and champagne for me? Who would tell my parents, who would deal with my body, who would care for my cats, who would handle my literary estate, who would finish all the unfinished work on my computer and make my orphaned dreams became books and films?

*"Now he would never have the chance to finish it,"* Hemingway (1961, p. 5) muses about his alter ego's imminent demise in "The Snows of Kilimanjaro." *"Now he would never write the things he had saved to write until he knew enough to write them well..."*

Those words have always haunted me.

*"Well,"* Hemingway (1961, p. 5) continues, *"he would not have to fail at trying to write them either."*

I was terrified of my being the accidental hermit, holed away in my apartment for days, weeks, never leaving, ordering delivery, writing novels and screenplays[1], my only interaction with the world email, instant messages, and the telephone...was this way of life, the writer's existence, the wrong path to take?

Hemingway (1961, p. 10): *"It was not so much that he lied as there was no truth to tell."*

I was afraid that I had pushed too many people out of my life, either from anger, jealousy, or apathy.

I realized we can never have enough people, enough friends, enough loved ones—the 100 plus souls with bodies, inside this tiny church, was proof of that.

"Do not feel sad for her," the friend admonished those sitting and weeping.

An infant behind me went "gggahhhhhh," as if the sound was critical commentary.

"Goooooo," I replied to the infant.

We understood each other. Cindy would have nodded in approval, lit a cigarette, and poured more white wine into her cup.

"Ghhheeeee," she would have said.

Someone said, "Feel sad for you, for the person sitting next to you, because Cindy is no longer standing by their side, but she is in their hearts, my heart, your heart, there she is, forever."

Cindy would have responded, "Oh, jeez Louise, so *sappy!*"

She would have said, "You need to get some help."

She would have said, "Pass the bottle," like the wind howling up from a seashell.

## DISCUSSION

I title this paper *anthropology of the memorial*; as a personal writing, it can also be labeled self-conscious anthropology (Cohen, 1992) as well as narrative sociology (Maines, 1993) along with auto/ethnography, since the subject matter is about observing myself interacting in a cultural ritual and arriving to an epiphany in the process. Ellis (2004) advocates the epiphany, or the transformation that occurs when learning something new about one's self, in auto/ethnographic accounts. Denzin (1989, p.22) claims epiphany is also necessary in the *mystory*, which

> is deeply entrenched in Western thought. At least since Augustine, the idea of transformation has been a central part of the autobiographical and biographical form. This means that [auto/ethnographic] texts will typically be structured by the significant, turning points moments in a subject's life.

I did indeed have my epiphany, perhaps several, at the memorial: I realized I had to stop being a social hermit, that I had to stop pushing people out of my life, that I needed less painful experiences and more joyful ones, that Cindy's friends who once criticized me for sleeping with her accepted me here, and all was okay, all was forgiven in their reality. This made me feel better, made me feel less guilty. When I first arrived at to the event, I had a feeling I was a bad person for the way I unemotionally interacted with Cindy in the past; at the end of the memorial, those feelings were washed away, the ways sins sometimes are in churches, in belief.

If the memorial had a more structured religious bent—say, Jewish or Catholic—if it happened in another country and culture, where the rules of the ritual had different parameters, would my experience have been the same? Denzin (1989) contends the epiphany is a Western experience, possibly with undertones of psychoanalysis, postmodernism, even poststructuralism. Different cultural data would inevitably yield different results. My method and approach would certainly not have been the same. The auto/ethnographer uses the personal lived experience as qualitative social data, unlike the traditional ethnographer that use the data of the other, or quantitative sets of data. Addressing this "us vs. them" situation, Ellis and Bochner (2006, p. 431) state that the auto/ethnographic method is clearly different than

> the work of the analytical ethnographers. We think of ethnography as a journey; they think of it as a destination. They want to master, explain, grasp. Those may be interesting word games, but we don't think they're necessarily important. Caring and empathizing is for us what abstracting and controlling is for them [...] we want to dwell in the flux of lived experience; they want to appropriate lived experience for the purpose of abstracting something they call knowledge or theory.

The anthropologist can double as an author (Geertz, 1988) which is what I am in this account. I have engaged in anthropological self-inscription (Reed-Donahay, 1997) as the attending ethnographer, observing myself and those around me, to understand the meaning behind this ritual and experience personal change through the process. Indeed, I was transformed by attending and transformed again by writing about it, which is one of the goals of auto/ethnography (Ellis, 2004), that the act of writing, and re-experiencing an event through words, can alter a person's perspective on the self.

How did the other people at the memorial see me, as Van Mannen (1988) posits is a reflective requisite for the confessional tale? I believe those I interacted with could see the transformation that was going on inside me as I experienced the social event. There were two rituals happening at Cindy's memorial—the outer of the attendees and the inner for myself. I did not want to go to the memorial for personal reasons, yet wound up feeling good that I was there. I walked away from it healed; I walked away with a smile on my face, not tears in my eyes, and I was not the only one aware of this. The next day, Giggles called and said, "I think it was a good thing that you participated."

Further accounts in qualitative research, this act of auto/ethnography, are published in increased quantities in various journals every year, from both the social sciences and humanities; more special journal issues crop up, book-length auto/ethnographies and anthologies are available from publishers, revealing that auto/ethnography is a popular, growing method of examining one's self in one's culture (Reed-Donahay, 1997). Auto/ethnography still has its opponents and critics, yet is embraced across a broader academic spectrum than it was fifteen, twenty years ago. Auto/ethnography is evidence of the changing nature in the many disciplines it is found in. Like any method, parameters and approaches will alter as auto/ethnography continues to develop through fresh and vibrant research.

## Notes

1. Before auto/ethnography became a common, popular term, qualitative researches described their personalized work, invariably, as first person sociology, alternative ethnography, auto-anthropology, reflexive ethnography, radical empiricism, and so on.
2. Hayano has been credited with coming up with the term auto/ethnography; his original notions, however, do not reflect the auto/ethnography commonly written today.
3. Fictional names are used.

# References

Behar, R. (1991). Death and memory: From Santa Maria del Monte to Miami Beach. *Cultural Anthropology, 6*(3), 346-384.

Behar, R. (1996) *The vulnerable observer: Anthropology that breaks your heart.* Boston: Basic Books.

Berg, L.V. & Trujillo, N. (2008). *Cancer and death: A love story in two voices.* Cresskill, NJ: Hampton Press.

Cary, L. J. (1999). Unexpected stories: Life history and the limits of representation. *Qualitative Inquiry, 5*(3), 411-427.

Coffey, A. (1999). *The ethnographic self.* London: Sage.

Cohen, Anthony P. (1994). *Self-consciousness: An alternative anthropology of identity.* NewYork: Routledge.

Conquergood, D. (1985). Performing as a moral act: Ethical dimensions of the ethnography of performance. Literature in Performance, 5, 1-13.

Carver, R. (1976). "Put yourself in my shoes." *Will you please be quiet, please?* NY: McGraw-Hill.

Denzin, N.K. (1989). *Interpretive biography.* Newbury Park: Sage.

Denzin, N.K. (1997). *Interpretive ethnography.* Newbury Park, CA: Sage.

Denzin, N.K. (2003). *Performance ethnography: critical pedagogy and the politics of culture.* Thousand Oaks: Sage.

Durham, D. (2005). Did you bathe this morning? Baths and morality in Bostwana. In Masquelier, A. (ed.), *Dirt, undress, and difference: critical perspectives on the body's surface.* Bloomington: Indiana University Press.

Ellis, C. (1991a). Sociological introspection and emotion experience. *Symbolic Interaction, 14*, 23-50.

Ellis, C. (1991b). Emotional sociology. *Studies in Symbolic Interaction, 12*, 123-145.

Ellis, C. (1993). "There are survivors": Telling a story of sudden death. *Sociological Quarterly, 34*, 711-730.

Ellis, C. (1995). Final negotiations. Philadelphia: Temple University Press.

Ellis, C. (1998). Exploring loss through autoethnographic inquiry: Autoethnographic stories, co-constructed narratives, and interpretive interviews. In J. H. Harvey (Ed.), *Perspectives on loss: A sourcebook* (pp. 49-62). Philadelphia: Taylor and Francis.

Ellis, C. (2004). *The ethnographic I.* Walnut Creek: AltaMira.

Ellis, C. & Bochner, A. P. (1996). *Composing ethnography: Alternative forms of qualitative writing.* Walnut Creek, CA: AltaMira Press.

Ellis, C. & Bochner, A. P. (2000). Autoethnography, personal narrative, reflexivity: Researcher as subject. In N. K. Denzin & Y. S. Lincoln (Eds.), *Handbook of qualitative research* (2nd ed., pp. 733-768). Thousand Oaks, CA: Sage.

Ellis, C. & Bochner, A.P. (2006) Analyzing analytic autoethnography: an autopsy. *Journal of Contemporary Ethnography, 35*(4), 429-449.

Garfinkel, H. (1969). *Studies in ethnomethodology.* Englewood: Prentice-Hall.

Geertz, C. (1973). *The interpretation of cultures.* NY: Basic Books.

Geertz, C. (1988).*Work and lives: The anthropologist as author.* Cambridge, UK: Polity.

Gorfain, P. (1986). Play and the problem of knowing in *Hamlet*: An excursion into interpretive anthropology. In Turner, V. & Bruner, E.M. (Eds.), *The anthropology of experience*. Illinois: University of Illinois Press.

Gubrian, J. (1988). *Analyzing field reality*. Newbury Park: Sage.

Haland, E.J. (2008). *Women, Pain and Death: Rituals and Everyday Life on the Margins of Europe and Beyond*. Newscastle-on-Tyne, UK: Cambridge Scholars.

Hayano, D.M. (1979). Auto-ethnography. *Human Organization, 38,* 99-104.

Hayano, D.M. (1982). *Poker faces*. Berkeley: University of California Press.

Hemingway, E. (1961). *The snows of Kilimanjaro*. NY: Charles Scribner's Sons.

Humphreys, M. (2005). Getting personal: Reflexivity and Autoethnographic vignettes. *Qualitative Inquiry, 11*(6), 840-860.

Kapferer, B. Performance and the structuring of meaning in experience. In Turner, V. & Bruner, E.M. (Eds.), *The anthropology of experience*. Illinois: University of Illinois Press.

Kolker, A. (1996). Thrown overboard: The human costs of health care rationing. In Ellis, C. & Bochner, A. P. (Eds.), *Composing ethnography: Alternative forms of qualitative   writing*. Walnut Creek, CA: AltaMira Press.

Lee, K.V. (2006) A fugue about grief. *Qualitative Inquiry, 12*(6), 1154-1159.

Lee, K.V. (2007) Georgie's girl: Last conversations with my father. *Journal of Social Work Practice, 21*(3), 289-296.

Meade, M. (1928). *Coming of age in Samoa*. NY: William Morrow.

Mills, C.W. (1959). *The sociological imagination*. New York: Oxford University Press.

Patton, M. Q. (2002). *Qualitative research and evaluation methods.* Thousand Oaks, CA: Sage.


Poulos, C. (2008). Narrative conscience and the autoethnographic adventure. *Qualitative Inquiry, 14*(1), 44-66.

Reed-Donahay, D. (1997). *Auto/Ethnography.* New York: Berg.

Resaldo, R. (1986). Ilongot hunting as story and experience. In Turner, V. & Bruner, E.M. (Eds.), *The anthropology of experience.* Illinois: University of Illinois Press.

Ronai, C.R. (1997). On loving and hating my mentally retarded mother. *Mental Retardation, 35,* 417-432.

Saldana, J., ed. (2005). *Ethnodrama: an anthology of reality theatre.* Lanham, MD: AltaMira.

Stewart, J. (1986). Patronage and control in the Trinidad carnival. In Turner, V. & Bruner, E.M. (Eds.), *The anthropology of experience.* Illinois: University of Illinois Press.

Van Mannen, J. (1988). *Tales of the field.* Chicago: University of Chicago Press.

# PROMISES MADE TO HEAVEN...BROKEN

## INTERPRETIVE AUTO/BIOLOGY AND THE
## AUTO/ETHNOGRAPHIC ACCOUNT

> You who do not remember
> passage from the other world
> I tell you I could speak again: whatever
> returns from oblivion returns
> to find a voice:
> >        ---Louise Glück, "The Wild Iris"

A friend of a friend was conducting interviews for her doctoral dissertation on pain that never heals; experiences so traumatic and hurtful that nothing, even time—the concept that allegedly, eventually, heals all—does not help bring peace to mind or soul.

This is what the friend of my friend was looking for: human data on personal pain that can last forever, the interpretive biography called a lifetime. I was uncomfortable about being a subject, but I am always happy and willing to help out a fellow anthropologist, sociologist, psychologist, and writer in collecting needed information.

> Interviewer: What hurts you and will always hurt you, no matter what?

Me: What has left a hole in my heart?"

Interviewer: A hole that will not heal, yes.

Me: A wound that always bleeds, like Lancelot's love for Guenivere, the betrayal against his friend and king...that would be fatherhood.

Interviewer: Your father?

Me: No, *that* one has healed...I'm talking about *being* a father...

## PERSONAL RELATIONSHIPS:
## AN AUTO/ETHNOGRAPHIC METHOD

This essay is an auto/ethnographic account about spiritual and metaphysical beliefs; the ideas and stories within the narrative are concerned with procreation in the 21st Century, the desire and need for fatherhood as men get older (that is to say, men have biological clocks as much as women) and the interaction and meaning of promises, lies, and betrayal in personal relationships. Subjectively, I address moral and ethical implications of when one person makes a promise to another—in this case, an important promise for the life of a child. The essay was inspired by the research the friend of a friend was engaged in, as previously noted. The technique I use is first person sociology (Kolker, 1995) and the format is the layered account (Ronai, 1992, 1995); my method is sociological introspection (Ellis, 1991) to present my experiences and emotions, looking back as I came to terms with a physical, spiritual, and emotional need to experience fatherhood.

This essay it also an account of spirituality, metaphysics, the belief in reincarnation, and a search for truth. At the core of auto/ethnography is the autobiographer's search for personal and cultural truth. What is auto/ethnography? Holt (2003: 3) explains it as

> a genre of writing and research that connects the personal to the cultural, placing the self within a social context (Reed-Danahay, 1997). These texts are usually written in the first person and feature dialogue, emotion, and self-consciousness as relational and institutional stories affected by history, social structure, and culture (Ellis & Bochner, 2000). Reed-Danahay explained that autoethnographers may vary in their emphasis on *graphy* (i.e., the research process), *ethnos* (i.e., culture), or *auto* (i.e., self). Whatever the specific focus, authors use their own experiences in a culture reflexively to look more deeply at self-other interactions. By writing themselves into their own work as major characters, autoethnographers have challenged accepted views about silent authorship, where the researcher's voice is not included in the presentation of findings.

Autobiographical "texts are written and read as if they have central cores of meaning [and] center a person at the heart of the life story" (Denzin 1989). The heart of this essay is about the human need to continue the next culture, to create the next generation of society, to contribute to the future.

# A Previous Loss <=> A Memory Sidebar[1]

In 1988, when I was twenty-two, I was in love and she was eight weeks pregnant. We decided we were going to have the baby, maybe get married. These were my "goth" days and I played guitar and wrote the music in a band called Tyburn Jig. We cut one LP that did not do so great, toured up and down the West Coast for a few months. I wanted to experience what it was like to be in a band (I had been playing guitar since I was fourteen, obsessed with Jimi Hendrix and Jimmy Page) and I would not trade those two years for anything, except for the death of Trudi and our baby. Trudi was a singer in another band; she had purple-dyed hair and wrote suicidal poetry/song lyrics, pale and 102 pounds, five-foot-five, it was love at first sight for both of us, or so we both liked to remember. It probably was not that "romantic" but it's what we liked to tell people. Now we were going to be three. "I never thought I could be so happy," she told me one night, the night I followed her car in my car (we both had cheap, run down cars, because we were both poor, starving musicians) and watched her— my life—die. A drunk driver in a big white truck (my white whale) ran a red light at seventy miles an hour and smashed into her little car, pushing it against the wall of a nearby convenience store. The sound of it sounded unreal, surreal, painful, the destruction of machines, metal wrapping around metal, and slicing into flesh. Trudi was cut in two from her midchest. Her death caused me to mentally and emotionally (and spiritually) shut down and I became homeless for a couple of years because I could not work and make money and I did not care. I died with her that night; the young man I was died with his companion and the fetus inside her and that man is a stranger to me, I remember him, and all the things he wanted and desired, but he is fading away from me every year; but every year I still go to her grave on that date and talk to her, I talk about the life we could have had. "We could have been grandparents by now," I say.

# A Biological Call

Reaching my late 30s, I thought a great deal about being a father, wondering if I could do it, wondering if I truly wanted it.

I had almost been a father a couple of times—when I was seventeen, twenty-two, and twenty-nine. A miscarriage, an abortion, and the death of the mother via car accident put a stop to those possible alternate personal timelines.

There were no pregnancies in my thirties. I thought a great deal about having a child, though, because I sensed a presence around me now and then. Call it a spirit, a ghost, a wish, a dream. A young boy would sit next to me and speak softly, telling me he wanted to be with me, telling me one day he *would be with me*, telling me his mother wasn't ready but she would be, *soon*, and she would come into my life. He told me she had made him a promise, a promise he expected her to keep, a promise only I could help her fulfill, a plan the three of us had agreed on before coming down to the planet for the lives we were experiencing now.

I write fiction. Sometimes my characters talk to me; sometimes they haunt me, any hour of the day and in my dreams. So I decided this boy child, this son, was from my imagination—*and he was*, he was from my mind, and I was soon to learn he was from Heaven, and I was not completely imagining all this, but every new life begins with a thought, a desire, and with love—and that thought manifests into a reality, the same way a novel or a film or a painting goes from thought to object, so does the creation of a child.

I will assign the term "auto/biology" for this calling and need to procreate. Auto/biology was used by Payne (1994: 49-50) as a means of writing that is

> concerned with the location of the body [...] "Autobiology" revisits a "concrete way of life," a past site of my own personal experience and asks (as well as I am able) what ways love, knowledge and power were constructed for me, through me, and by me [...] How was

my body located in this situation? [...] Can I somehow reclaim the site of my body and narrate my experience on my own terms?

Similarly, this account places my body in a time and place in my life, culture, and the society I am part of and the conflicts of such with an emotional and physical desire to become a father. It is a curious thing, the extent to which people will go when the auto/biogical call motivates them; in an auto/ethnographic account, Neville-Jan (2004: 113) explains her journey to motherhood as selling her soul to the devil because she is disabled and "experienced three years of severe, unremitting neurogenic pain," yet for all her suffering, she felt it was necessary and worthwhile.

## A PRE-BIRTH CALLING

There is a long history in folklore, literature, and metaphysical theory that souls contact one or both parents (usually the mother more than the father) months if not years before conception and birth (Hallett and Carmen, 2000). It has become an area of human communications studies for paraphychologists and psychologists alike. "The unborn child communicates not only with its mother, but with receptive people in its environment who may find themselves cast in the role of interpreters or message-carriers" (Moss, 2000: 171).

> These receptive people [are] "soul-helpers," and the information they receive is often about a needed change to benefit mother and/or child, such as adding more protein to the mother's diet. Sometimes the message is more like an announcement, as if the soul is introducing itself to a third person who will carry the news to the parents. Through these interactions with an "outsider," independ-

ent of any physical connection, the unborn soul adds weight to the evidence that it exists (Hallett, 2002b, online).

Hallett suggests that the number of pre-birth and pre-conception contact with the souls of future children is increasing.

> Some experiences are dramatic; some are subtle and fleeting. And some [...] are life-changing [...] [which] leads us to consider the reality of life before birth, and even the possibility of existence before conception. We glimpse patterns and meanings that may change our very ideas of life and death. The way we see our children may also begin to change. Suppose that our children existed *before* this life they share with us -- what are the implications? (Hallett, 2002a, online).

The origins of the experiences and emotions I address in this paper are a result from a pre-life and pre-birth communication from a spirit I nicknamed "Pabst." I gave him that name because when my physic advisor "saw" him, she described his spirit as "being like a dancing blue ribbon, circling about you and his mother." Yes, I nicknamed him after a cheap beer product.

## A PSYCHIC CALLING

Sometimes I seek counsel from psychics. Many people do but few will admit it. We do this when we feel lost and confused. We live in a world with the fear of fate—especially writers. Sometimes the psychics help, sometimes they make things worse, sometimes what is said changes nothing and it is all a waste of money. Sometimes they are *right on the money* and you marvel at it, you wonder *how* they knew; they make predictions and two months later it happens, or that predicted

34

person shows up, and you are convinced of the authenticity, so you go back and pay more money for more metaphysical insights.

I crossed paths with a psychic named Nancy; she had a storefront across the street from Horton Plaza, a mall in downtown San Diego. I paid her $65 for a half-hour reading. She told me some interesting things. She said I had to break up with the woman I was living with, but to "make it right." It was important that things were "right" and I had to leave her to make room for a woman I was destined to have two children with, two sons, and possibly marry; whether we married or not, we would have at least one of the sons, possibly two, and later I would have a daughter with another, younger woman. But for now, there was this woman.

"Who is she?" I asked.

"You know her," Nancy said.

"I do?"

"She's from your past, you haven't spoken to her in a while, but you need to contact her."

"What's her name?"

"Right now, all I see is blonde hair."

That was 60% of the women I knew or once knew.

Three weeks later, I was walking downtown near Horton Plaza and heard my name repeatedly called.

It was Nancy.

She ran up to me, grabbing my sleeve, out of breath. "I'm so happy you're here," she said; "I didn't have your number or any way to contact you. I have something important to tell you."

"Oh," I said, leery of the sales pitch. "How much will it cost?" I asked.

"Nothing," she said. "God told me I have to help you I am not allowed to charge you."

I didn't get it.

"You have something very important to do," she said, "important for the world."

"Really. What do I have to do?"

"Not *you*," she said. "Your *son*," she said.

## A MYSTERY FOR SOLVING

"Your job," Nancy said, back at her storefront, the Tarot cards laid on the table like troops ready to siege a fort, "your *karmic mission*, your *spiritual agreement*, is to raise this child so he can complete his mission."

"Mission," I said.

"I'm not sure what it is, exactly; all I can say is the boy will be a prodigy, he will marvel and maybe even scare people—he will walk and talk at six months, he will pick up reading, writing, and playing musical instruments by the time he is two. The mother will not know what to do with this kind of child but you will, you will teach him and help him." She frowned, seemed troubled. "That isn't to say it will be easy. It can never be easy with a gifted star child. He will have health problems, he will be sickly when he is very young and there will be close calls and you and the mother will fear for his life, the problem may even pull you and the mother apart because she will blame you. So you must pay attention to his health, and get him to the hospital quickly whenever there is a problem. After he is five or six, there will be no more health issues and he will be fine. It's those early years that will be difficult and trying for you and the mother; you two just need to get through it to make way for the second child."

"Another one."

"Another boy," she said; "he is not for certain. He wants to come through but things are not set yet. The first son must be born, *has* to be born, is *meant* to be, and the world needs him a much as he needs the world. First, though, you must contact the mother and start a relationship with her."

"I don't know who she is," I said; "I don't know who you're talking about."

"You will," Nancy said, "oh you will—it was written to be so. And she's your soul mate; if you don't find her she'll find you. That could take a while, it is better that you find her first. I should say 're-find' her. Oh, come on, Michael," she said, "you must know who this blonde woman is."

"I don't."

She dealt another hand of the cards, to give her insight into this mysterious mother of my children. "She lives with guilt and pain—she feels she has let her family down, and herself down. Many opportunities were handed to her, doors were opened, but she failed to act. She feels trapped. She feels uncomfortable in her body, as a human—she has not had many lives on Earth. Her soul is close to the angelic order—an old soul, but flawed, here to redeem herself with an important mission that she is at risk of failing. She is living the wrong life. Your job is to steer her to the right life. You both made a pre-life agreement on certain matters. She is one of your soul mates, and you have had many lives together, on this world and others.

"Because she feels alien to this world and life," Nancy went on, "she has problems with alcohol and drugs. She has emotional issues. Her heart is scarred from the past. She thinks about suicide a lot. She may have tried to kill herself when she was younger."

## A POSSIBLE MOTHER

One night, I had a dream about Kelly Greene.[*]

Kelly was an actress whom I had cast in a couple of my short plays in a local theater festival. I had auditioned her a couple of times at my former theater company where I was Literary Manager for five years, running the company with my ex-girlfriend, who was now in New York, married, with a daughter. Kelly also had a daughter. She was a single mother, divorced. I was always attracted to her, was from the first time she came to an audition—she was a tall, beautiful blonde; a cross between Darryl Hannah and Laura Dern and Uma Thurman, all tall, awkward, and gorgeous blondes. Although I was attracted to Kelly, I was afraid of her. I do not usually like women my height or taller. Kelly stood five foot ten and I am five-eleven; with heels she was taller than me. She seemed to be angry a lot. Her anger terrified me, as if she were going to explode at any moment into an epicenter of violence.

One time at rehearsal I had joked about who would marry me and become my future ex-wife. Kelly said, "I'll marry you!" I didn't know if she was serious or joking. I know she was curious about me—at the time, I had been directing many plays in town, and she was an actress in need of resume credits. She had also been an English major, was interested in writing, and I was a published author; in fact, at the time, my agent was negotiating the publication of my first genre hardback with a commercial publisher, *Wild Turkey* (2001a). When the play went up, I had won a $6,000 grant for

---

[*] I have changed her name. "Kelly Green" is the pen name we had chosen for a collaborative young adult novel that we never finished, let alone published. I keep telling myself that one of these days I will finish it alone.

my novel-in-progress, *The Rose of Heaven* (2004), and received a $25,000 advance for an anthology with my British publisher (2001b). To an outsider, to Kelly in particular, I had the social appearance of a successful author and playwright. There was some flirtation between us but I didn't pursue Kelly. I called her on the phone now and then, always wondering if I made a mistake, if I should have explored a relationship. I felt a connection with her, "a feeling of familiarity" that Nancy said came from the two of us being together in many past lives, as spouses, siblings, best friends, even enemies, the way (some believe) soul mates interact throughout time.* I had not talked to her in two years except during the staged reading she did of one of my plays, "Milk" (2007).

Then I had a dream about her. In the dream, we were at a party together, with her daughter; it was a party at a big house that for some reason I thought was mine, or ours— Kelly and I were together in this dream, maybe married, but we were a couple and this was possibly our house, and all our friends and family were there, celebrating something.

---

* There is also the theory that we have more than one "soul mate," these being souls that form a "soul group." Thus, we could have several kindred souls from the same group come in and out of our lives. There is also the belief that our true soul mates, or "twin soul," never incarnate together; one will act as a spirit guide for the other in life durations. If these twin souls do incarnate as the same time, it is often not bliss, true love, and heaven on earth; twin souls, in human form, are often antagonistic and take the role of the rival nemesis, or enemy. The souls are too much alike to get along as humans; the negative relationship is often on purpose for one karmic or cosmic reason or another. In this case, I began to believe that Kelly and I (she often said she felt a soul mate kinship with me) had incarnated for the purpose of being parents to this boy child, to raise him and make sure he completed whatever his mission was on earth; I believed that all our dreams and goals for art and acting and film were secondary to the co-parenting of the child.

I woke up from the dream confused. I had not thought about Kelly in a year. Last I knew, she was with this bartender named Rick and it seemed to be serious. I got out of bed, troubled by this dream. I went to the living room and turned on the television. It was 3:30 a.m.

Kelly was on the TV.

She was on the TV and wearing the same clothes in my dream—a large button down shirt over a t-shirt, and jeans.

It was a commercial for a local bail bonds company; the commercial had been running for three years, usually late at night during *Star Trek* and *X-Files* reruns. In the commercial, she is lying in bed and is awaked by the telephone. In the background a baby is crying. On the phone, a man says he has been arrested, he's in jail, he needs her to bail him out. *"Jail!?"* she says in a high-pitch tone I would later come to know all too well. The scene cuts to an exterior of the bail bond office, and then cuts to the interior. She has processed the paperwork to get her husband out of the slammer. She smiles warmly and says, "Thank you."

I had a dream about her, and then there she was, on TV.

Was she the one?

I sent her an email. She replied, saying we should have coffee and catch up—*Or should we skip the coffee and go straight to the tequila?*

*Remember when you said you would marry me*, I wrote to Kelly; *do you still want to?*

*I've given up on men*, she wrote back, *I think I'll be a lesbian now.*

# A CONNECTION

I casually corresponded with Kelly for many months, not knowing what to do. I told Nancy about Kelly; she shuffled the cards and said, "Yes, this Kelly is *the one*, she is the *mother of your son*." I did not know how that could be. I hardly knew her, for one, except when we worked on the plays, but I didn't know her well, and I no longer found her attractive. Her eyes were always angry or sad, or both. She was abrasive with her words, judgmental and harsh. She was also in her 30s now, still working the 9-to-5 and not the famous actress she dreamed to be. I have had significant experience with actresses—and once they reach 30, the fact that they are not on the cover of *Vogue* and accepting awards for their movies hits them hard; they become bitter, mad, sad, and frustrated, looking to place blame on the men they are with—men who have held them back, who were not supportive. When I was directing plays, the actresses I dated expected me to cast them in every play. Actresses, I have come to understand, do not accept the fact that they are not right for every role—sometimes they are, sometimes not.

Kelly was always being cast as the "tough chick" or the lesbian. She wanted bigger, better, more varied roles, but they weren't coming, and she hadn't been doing many mainstage shows; just festivals, staged readings, short runs with small companies. This was not what she wanted; this was not what she envisioned herself when reaching her 30s. The fact that she was not in movies, and famous in some way, and was still struggling to make ends meet, was eating away at her soul.

# A Near Death Experience...
# A Metaphysical Sidebar

*Something happened during that time period.*

*I died on October 20, 2004.*

*At 4:00 a.m., drifting off to sleep, my heart stopped. It was like a giant hand had reached into my chest and squeezed. It was a sensation I never want to feel again.*

*Then I was floating near the ceiling, looking down at my body, the body that was still and dead on the bed.*

*I did not "go into the light" but next I was somewhere else, some other realm, where it was peaceful and...heavenly. I felt at peace, I felt love. I saw Kelly there, but she was "in limbo," a sleeping-walking state souls have when they are experiencing a life on earth. She did not look like the physicals Kelly—it is difficult to explain, she as a shimmering ball of golden white light, and I simply "new" it was her. I cannot even say if she had a gender, but this soul belonged to the woman named Kelly Greene down on earth.*

*My time in this space felt like two weeks. I sat around, relaxing, enjoying the peace. I was waiting.*

*Waiting for my life review.*

*Next I was in a large hall, surrounded by tall beings in white robes. The Masters. I had read about them, I knew who they were.*

*There would be no life review.*

*They said I had to go back.*

*They said I had a mission to fulfill.*

**I said I didn't want to return.**

*They said I had to. They said I had no choice.*

*I said what about free will.*

42

*Free will is a philosophy of the flesh, I was told. In this case, I was told, I had to return and complete my karmic agreement with Kelly and our son.*

*I was approached by a soul. He was very tall, very powerful, I had known him for all eternity. I knew he was, in the past, my guide, my master, my friend. He transformed into a small boy, about five years old.*

*Father, he said, I will take you back so I can be born.*

*He took my hand and together, we fell to the earth.*

*I am afraid, I said.*

*Don't be, he said.*

*I re-entered my body. I didn't know how, or how I know, but this child soul did something to my heart, he stimulated it with his own energy, and my heart started beating again.*

*I sat up, gasping, clutching at my chest.*

*In world time, my heart had stopped for perhaps fifteen or thirty seconds.*

> The child was standing in front of me,
> in the bedroom.
>
> He smiled, and then vanished.
>
> There was a slight pain in my chest.
>
> To this day, my heart still beats oddly.
>
> I knew that if I did not complete this mission, my heart would stop again
> and I would be sent home.

## AN EFFORT TO CONNECT

Kelly sent me an email saying that she went to a family gathering in Hawaii for Thanksgiving. "The whole time there and back I cried on the plane," she told me, "because I can never keep my promises or stick to my plans. I feel like a failure."

I didn't ask why, but a year later I would know why.

We had a few drinks together one night. I watched her every move, trying to determine if she was the one. She said, "Something strange happened that made me think of you. My daughter and I were walking by the shore the other night, and we saw a shimmering, glowing figure walking by the water. It was blue and translucent, and looked like a human. It was a ghost or an alien. My daughter was scared; she wanted to run away. I wanted to watch it. It walked into the water and disappeared. Just like that—vanished."

"You were meant to see it," I said. "What do you think the message was? *Who* do you think it was?"

In my heart, I felt it had something to do with the child.

"I think it was my grandfather," she said. "I have been trying to contact him. I need to talk to him. I think it was him."

"What was he trying to tell you?" I asked.

"...not sure."

"Walking into the ocean..."

"Maybe a journey..."

"The vastness of the ocean..."

"I wish I knew," she said.

"..."

"Do you know?" she asked.

"No," I lied.

On Christmas Eve, she he came by my apartment. We were both alone. "Let's be alone together," I suggested. After a couple of drinks at a bar, we went back at my apartment and I tried to kiss her.

She avoided me. "I have to go."

I was rejected and it didn't feel good.

She called a few minutes later from her cell phone. "I'm sorry," she said. "For what almost happened, for running away," she said. "I'm just not into that right now. A different time, sure, I like having fun; but not right now," she said.

I went to Nancy for advice; I told her I didn't think Kelly was the one—she had turned down my advance, and I had admit I didn't find her all that attractive—I didn't like how she dressed or smelled.

"No," Nancy said; "she *is* the one."

"She rejected me."

"You know nothing about women. They like to be pursued. You need to be persistent, keep at it; she needs to *know* you're serious."

## A METAPHYSICAL EXPERIENCE

We had dinner at a German restaurant down the street from where I lived. The place had great happy hour food and a large selection of German beers. Tipsy, she became melancholy and remorseful. She started to cry. I held her. The TV in the restaurant was turned to the Grammy Awards. A song came on about daughters and fathers. "That song always makes me cry," she said, and she cried more, because the song reminded her that her ex-husband was a lousy father to her child. She talked about regrets and how hard it was to be a single mother. "Look what my life is, because I happened to screw the *wrong guy*." She didn't blame her daughter; she loved that child and knew it was right to have her instead of getting an abortion. The custody agreement with the father, however, didn't allow her to take the kid out of San Diego. "I'm stuck here," Kelly said, "I'm trapped in my life." She was a theater actress but didn't have time to do more than one or two shows a year, because she had to work and tend to the needs of her family; and because she couldn't move from San Diego with her daughter, she couldn't explore a life in Los Angeles as an actress.

I asked: "What is it that you really, truly want? Tell me, and I'll get it for you."

She said: "To be an actress in independent films."

"I can do that," I said. My professional writing career included many published novels, stories, articles and plays; while I'd optioned a couple of my books that were never fully developed, I never sat down to write screenplays. I knew that I would write them, eventually, and *now* seemed the right time. "I'll write screenplays for us both to do," I said, "we'll produce them low budget and get Hollywood's attention, and we'll be filmmakers."

She was too drunk to drive home; she was too drunk to walk down the street. She held onto my arm, giggling. She asked if she could sleep on my couch. I was hoping she'd ask to sleep in my bed. I thought of making a move, to try to kiss her again, but she simply was too drunk. I don't like to be intimate with women that drunk—you can never be certain if they actually like you, if they're pretending you're someone else; and the morning can be awkward, especially if they do not remember anything. Drunken sex can lead to never speaking to one another again.

I gave her a bottle of water. I sat next to her. We watched some TV. I wanted to kiss her; I was afraid to kiss her; I was afraid to touch her.

"...sleep now," Kelly said, closing her eyes.

I went to the bedroom and got her a blanket and a pillow. She was asleep and in her sleep she hugged the pillow. I was jealous of the pillow. She had opened the button of her jeans to let her stomach breathe. Her bellybutton was pieced with a small jewel. Her skin was pink.

I sat at my desk, behind my computer, which was next to the couch. I watched her sleep. She looked so peaceful. I noted how her jeans contoured around her vagina.

I could take her, I thought. I had known women who responded, when drunk, to being woken up for sex.

And then the spirit of the boy showed up.

He stood next to Kelly and said, *This is my mother.*

"I thought so," I said.

*This is my chosen mother, and you must help her keep her promise*, he said.

"What promise?"

> **She made a promise to heaven that she broke.**
> **She is torn up inside about it.**
> **I cannot come down here, inside her, if she is like that.**
> **I will be damaged.**
> **You must help her keep her promise so that I can be with you both.**
> **You must help her with her dreams so she will be happy.**

"Okay," I said, "I will do that."

This is why I did not try to have sex with her. Too much was at stake. I didn't want to scare her, hurt her, lose her—not if this child needed to be born. I would wait for her to make that move, that choice, of intimacy, so I would know that it was all right and we could do our job.

## CONFESSIONS

For the next two months, Kelly and I got together every Sunday, after she dropped off her daughter to her ex-husband; Sundays and Mondays were his days to have custody. We emailed each other every day—I usually had to initiate the communication; I'd email her at work, at home, or text her. If she was chosen as the mother of my child, or children, I had to get to know her better, she had to become use to talking to me on a daily basis. Also—despite the visitation—I still had my doubts; I questioned the reality of the experience, was

48

aware that it could have been in my anthropological imagination: that like any metaphysical vision, the vision could be self-created out of desire.

One Sunday, Kelly and I had lunch by the beach and we were drinking beer. We were drinking a lot of beer. Oh, we loved to drink, if that is not already obvious. "It's hard to match you beer for beer," she said; the end result is that we both got very drunk. Kelly decided to make a confession. "I'm going to tell you something and then I don't want to talk about it," she said.

"Okay," I said.

"I was once pregnant and today I was due to deliver," she said.

I didn't get it; took me half a minute to understand what that meant, to grasp what she was telling me. She was once pregnant, she isn't anymore—she was due today; so that meant nine months ago she had sex with someone, someone else. I could not ask her this because she said she didn't want to talk about it.

She knew I wanted to ask questions. "I guess it's hard *not* to talk about something like this," she said.

"What the hell happened?"

"This guy, some guy, I was seeing," she said, curling her lip, waving her hand. "After I broke up with him, a few weeks later I realized…what condition I was in."

I did the math in my head. We had been in contact when it happened; I was sending emails and calling, to see if Nancy was right. In fact, I realized she had the abortion around Thanksgiving—that's why she was crying on the plane back from Hawaii, that's why she had seen that spirit on the beach. I had no idea she was sleeping with someone then. That was painful; I felt betrayed but knew I had no reason to, there was no agreement between us, not then or now, and I had slept with two women in Los Angeles while I was making initial connections with Kelly. It was just recreational sex, and I knew this was the same for Kelly and whoever this man was; I knew she did not love him, that is why she broke up with him. I did not want to know who he was because I was afraid it was someone in the theater community, someone I might know.

"I promised myself I would never have an abortion again," she said, "because I know there is a soul who wants in, who has chosen me as its mother..."

I took her confession as a sign. Had she been visited too by Pabst the blue ribbon?

"The child is a boy," I said.

She nodded.

"He's been around you for some time."

She nodded.

"There is something very important he needs to do and only you can help him."

"I think so."

I asked, "Aren't you wondering how I know all this?"

She shrugged and smiled. "I always knew you had psychic powers."

I held her hand. She started to cry and I cried with her, because I felt the loss, I knew what was in her heart. We were drunk and the best way to numb the pain was to drink more. She confessed to me that it was her fifth abortion. "The first time, I was fifteen," she said, "if I had played my cards right, I'd have a child in college by now." She said the other times were with her husband and a boyfriend, and this most recent one with "some guy" she had been dating. I told her about the two I had.

In a drunken spur of the moment, she said she wanted to mark this day on her body and get a tattoo. We were by the beach and San Diego's beaches have a plethora of tattoo shops. We walked down the block to one, which proved to be somewhat difficult because we were so drunk we were having a hard time moving our legs. $40, a few minutes, and she had a new tattoo on her ankle: five small black dots. "Doop doop doop," she said, touching each one.

We went into a bar and had a few more drinks. She was too drunk to drive and we were too drunk to walk back to my apartment. There was a motel by the beach that I liked. "Well, two drunks burping, snoring, and farting," Kelly said, "how romantic." Then she started to cry. I paid for the room. Once in, she really let it out, hitting the bed, screaming for her five dead children, snot flying out of her nose and onto the wall. All I could do was hold her. I had no idea what else to do.

She got up, took off her slacks and blouse, went into the bathroom and took a shower. I could hear her giggling as the water splashed on her body. I was unsure if this was a signal. Did she want me to join her? In a romantic setting, that would be expected. But this was a scene of pain; there was no lust in the air. She returned to the room, a towel wrapped around her naked body, barely covering her vagina, I could see some blonde pubic hair sticking out. She lay on the bed and turned on the TV. I moved alongside her. She stared at the TV. I wanted to kiss her. I touched her arm.

"You wanted yours, didn't you?" she asked.

"Yes."

"Why didn't..."

I said, "The first time, we were teenagers, and—you know. The second time, we were poor starving theater artists.

We could barely take care of ourselves. But I think about them now and then."

"I think about mine all the time, and now I have the marks on my body—ploop ploop ploop." Then she started to cry again. She admitted to guilt, because after the fourth abortion, she said she made a silent and solemn promise that her son would be born, "come hell or high water," by 2005. "I think he's mad at me," she said, "for breaking that promise."

I knew there was not going to be sex between us. That was all right with me. I didn't want sex. I just wanted to be next to her and hold her. I did, and she fell asleep, her face pressed to my neck, her long blonde hair around my face and the pillows.

Pabst appeared, like I knew he would. He sat between us.

*Not now,* he said. *She isn't ready. You're not ready.*

He knew what I was thinking—that if I initiated sex while she was asleep, and still drunk, she would probably submit herself to my touch and I could get her pregnant.

In the middle of the warm summer night, I woke up with an erection because her naked skin was pressed into mine. The idea came to me again—I could make a move, I could impregnate her and get the ball rolling. But Pabst said this was not the right time. I got up, went to the bathroom, considered masturbation to get sex out of my mind. I splashed water on my face. In the room, on the bed, Kelly had turned so her towel fell off, and she was on her back, her legs spread open, her vagina in front of my face. Any other man, I suppose, would not have been able to resist, but seeing her like that, I was not sexually aroused; she was attractive, and sexy, and I admired her breasts, her legs, but my erection was gone and I had no desire or lust in me. I just wanted to

52

go back to sleep. I covered Kelly up and sat on the bed, watching her.

She was miserable in the morning; she had a bad hangover, which was to be expected. She seemed surprised that she was naked. "Did we...?" she said.

I shook my head.

"Good," she said.

I was upset, insulted—she had no idea if we had sex or not, and when I tell her no, she says, "Good"? What the hell was that?

Over the next few weeks, through e-mail and conversations, I brought up the issue of babies, children, karma, destiny. I was careful about revealing everything in layers. She knew what I was getting at. I told her what Nancy said, about Pabst, the "blue ribbon" spirit between us.

"We can't have a baby," she said; "you can barely take care of yourself."

Again, I was insulted. "How dare you," I said; "you're living at your mom's because you're so far in debt and I make more money than you, and I do it from home; I don't have a boss or answer to anyone but my publishers."

"I'm sorry."

"I was never going to tell you about the psychic reading, what I was told, and the boy spirit," I said. "If we ever had a child, I would have told you after he was born. But I was going to keep this a secret...until the other night...what you told me...I took it as a sign."

"A sign for what?"

"For why we are here, now," I said. "To give this soul his life and raise him so he can do whatever it is he needs to do."

## A SOLUTION TO AMEND GUILT:
## AN ACTIVE INTERVIEW

The following is from the interview I gave with the researcher mentioned at the top of this account.

> Interviewer: How did she react? I mean, speaking as a woman, that's a lot of pressure, to say, "We're destined to have this baby because we agreed to before this life and if we don't we're doomed."

> Me: That's what she felt. That's what she said. "You need saving," she said. I told her she did too. She said, "You can barely take care of yourself, how can you take care of a kid?" That was insulting. I told her she had no right to judge me because I made more money than she did. Plus, she and her daughter were living at her mother's house, and her mother was renting out an apartment, because Kelly was so deep in debt and could not afford the rising rent in their part of town.

> Interviewer: She could have moved.

> Me: No, the schools are good in that area, and she wanted her daughter to be in a decent school. She would have preferred a private school but she could not afford that. I said our son would never go to a public school, we would make sure he had the best education possible, because that was important.

> Interviewer: "Pabst"?

Me: That was his nickname. In the dream I had, when he came to me, he said his name was Gabriel. In the spirit world, anyway. I'm not sure if that would be his name when he was alive, born, had a body. I had a feeling that Kelly already had a name for him. I asked her if she did but she said no. I didn't believe her, I could see it on her face, plus I later learned she lied a lot. About little things. For no reason. Pathological, I guess. But that is something else.

Interviewer: You said she is bi-polar.

Me: Very much so. Crazy mood swings. One moment she would be happy and full of life, an hour later she would be suicidal and full of gloom. Plus she drank a lot—not all the time, from what I could tell, and then I started to realize she was drinking every night.

Interviewer: Not a good combination, with bi-polar disorder.

Me: I told her she would have to give up booze for the baby. That she had to get ready for that, for Pabst's sake.

Interviewer: What about post-partum depression…seems she would be at risk for that.

Me: Thought of that. And I was worried about it I figured I would deal with it when the time came. First things first. I mean, we'd never even had sex. Had to get that out of the way, and then the baby…

Interviewer: You have to admit, it's all kind of strange. You're not even together, haven't had sex, but you're asking her to have a child with you, and the two of you have named this person who doesn't even exits.

Me: Oh, he existed. He does exist. He's a person. He just doesn't have a body. He's s soul that feels and thinks and has a personality and is as real as you and me, he just exists in a different dimension, the spirit world, he just needed a body as a way of coming into this world. I felt love for him, I feel love for him now. I don't feel his presence much anymore, but at the time, I always felt him around. I felt it stronger when Kelly and I were together. When we went to the movies, drove around, or spent a few platonic nights together in bed, I could feel him there sitting between us, or bouncing back and forth, that "blue ribbon," and it was a strong, good, and loving feeling  I think I became addicted to that feeling. I wanted to be round Kelly more just so I could feel it. When she acted in a play, I would "see" him with her on stage, I would see that dancing blue ribbon wrapping itself around her body. All I can say is, it was beautiful to see, to feel, and I tried to explain this to her. She claimed she did not feel his presence but I know she did, I know she was lying, I know he was entering her dreams and I know she could feel him.

Interviewer: Why would she lie about that?

Me: Because it would validate my contention that he had chose us as parents and that it was important for him to be born, that we did this.

Interviewer: But she said no, she didn't want to…

Me: She wanted him. She wanted another baby. She always wanted to have "a house full of children," she said. She wanted, and needed, a new baby, but she was afraid; afraid she would have to do it alone, afraid she wouldn't have the money to raise him right, give him a good home. I assured it she had nothing to fear; I said I would never abandon her. Why would I deprive myself of the experience I was craving, that I needed in my life? I said I would go through the pregnancy every minute with her, because I wanted that experience in my life.

Interviewer: You felt the experience would fill the emptiness you felt…?

Me: …yes. I knew it would.

Interviewer: And what if it didn't…?

Me: I told her there would be plenty of money to do this, with pour combined incomes, and my selling screenplays. Things were slowly happening in Hollywood. A few of my novels had been optioned, I was getting meetings for my screenplays, it was only a matter of time. Once I set my mind onto something, I go and get it. I won't take no for an answer.

Interviewer: But she was saying "no."

Me: I was meeting resistance. I kept at her. I was not going to give up. No, I would not take "no" from her as an answer. Too much was at stake, this child's life, this person, I knew I had to fight for him and convince her. I told her this was the correct and perfect way for us both to make amends to the guilt we both felt, the abortions we'd both had. She wanted a new baby, I wanted a child, I said what was the problem. She finally agreed. She said I had to make some changes in my life as a condition, in the way I treated her, and she wanted me to lose some weight and take better care of myself. She couldn't impose change on me without her changing. I wanted her to stop smoking and drinking and get physically ready to be pregnant. I wanted her to stop being mean to me when she got into her dark moods. So we seemed to have an agreement; we'd do this; there was no timeframe but I said it'd have to be soon, within the next six months, no more than a year. And I was happy. I finally felt happy, and elated, that things would change...

Interviewer: That things would go your way...

Me: The right way, the way things had to be.

Interviewer: But...

Me: She started to pick fights with me. I think she was trying to find an excuse, to make things go bad. Near Christmas, she started to avoid me, to not come by my place. We mostly talked on the phone. She said, "I'm very sad these days and I am trying to figure out where to place it all." And then she said she was feeling suicidal whenever she thought of being married or together, and having this child. She said, "I can't do it." She said, "I'm not going to have a family with you."

Interviewer: Ouch.

Me: It hurt. Maybe the most hurtful words I have ever had said to me. How can you say that to a person...one month, it's "okay, we'll have the baby" and then "I'm not going to have a family with you." She said, "I'm sorry, I lied." She said, "I only agreed because I thought you'd kill yourself." She said, "You drive me crazy, how can I be with you, have a child with you?" I said, "You promised me, you promised Pabst." I said, "How can you break a promise like that?"

Interviewer: And she said...?

Me: She hung up the phone.

## LOSS AND TRAUMA

She said, "You'll get over it in time."

I said, "I will never forgive you."

She said, *"Forget* me instead."

I said, "I will never forgive you and neither will he."

She said, "Oh, Jesus, you've gone off the deep end with that."

I said, "You made a promise. To me. To him."

She said, "I have never kept a single promise in my life, you know that, so why are you surprised?"

When Kelly went back on her promise, the emotions I felt were the same as if a physical flesh-and-bone child of mine had died. I tried to tell myself this was "the death of an idea" or "the death of a dream" or "the death of the possibility of having a family," but what I experienced was emotional pain, depression, and devastating loss. I realized I was grieving. I felt like I wanted to die but I was not suicidal; I viewed death as a means to escape the agony I was in, and metaphysically, death would be a way to be with the soul who was now not going to receive his life. Along with emotional and spiritual pain, I was angry—I was angry at Kelly and at the Universe. I felt betrayed by Kelly, betrayed by God, betrayed by my own desire of fatherhood. I was angry with every person I saw in public who had an infant or small children, similar to the envy I witnessed on Kelly's face whenever she saw someone with a baby, and how she would always say, "I forgot they came in that size." I would walk to the post office or down to the beach and see many parents pushing strollers; the majority of these mothers and fathers, who were either alone or together with their infants, were young, in their late teens to mid twenties, and what I noticed was that each of them looked unhappy; they looked stressed, trapped, scared, confused. Their young lives had changed with the birth of a baby; all their hopes and dreams were moist likely derailed and they had economic worries, the usual burden of young parents. I looked at them and I felt jealousy and anger. I thought it was unfair—here were these people who were not happy being parents, who had second thoughts about keeping the pregnancies in their lives; they didn't want what they had, which is what I wanted. I asked myself why was this—why do people get something they wind up not wanting whereas someone like me, who desperately wanted it, could not have it? One friend told me, "Go out and knock some chick up." That was not the issue; I knew I could seek out a woman in the dating arena who wanted a family and I could do that, but that was not feasible. I only wanted Kelly to give me a child; I knew only she could be the mother. Believing that we choose our parents before we are born, I knew that Pabst would not enter his soul into the body of any child that was not in Kelly's womb; likewise, I knew that he would not enter any body that I did not father.

Because I was angry, I became verbally abusive toward Kelly. I sent her angry emails. How else could I respond to someone who had lied to me about the most important thing two people could agree on? Not only had Kelly destroyed the family we were to have, she destroyed our plans to make independent films and go to Hollywood.

When I finally did find a production company to option one of my screenplays, and a year later film it, the joy of having my first movie made was a lonely experience. Kelly was not there, with me, experiencing it with me, like we had planned on doing, with our son. I was alone and it was an empty victory, and every day on the set all I could think of was how wrong it felt, that Kelly should be here, and Pabst too. I felt like I was living the wrong life. I became angry again, *very angry*, with Kelly, for taking away what should have been a wonderful experience and making it an joyless one. Thousands of people go to Los Angeles with dreams of making movies but only a very small percentage ever actually get to do it, and I had accomplished this, I had fought for it, but the fight had always been intended for the sake of Pabst, to lay the foundations for his future.

I would call Kelly every day while on set. She never answered her phone. I did not want her to. I only wanted to leave messages for her so she would know how much pain I was in, and how I blamed her. I said mean things. I told her she had destroyed her chance at being an actress in films. I told her she had murdered our son and she should be ashamed.

And I was ashamed of myself for saying these things. Perhaps it was all petty.

I have taken into account the death of Trudi and our child when I was twenty-three, what now seems like another life ago, someone else's life, a narrative I have appropriated and is more like flashing images on a screen. The feelings are still there, the pain is still there, and the pain has grown, has haunted me more than I want to admit. That loss only amplified the loss I felt from Kelly's broken promise. It was the true pain that would never heal.

Ellis (1991, 2004) calls for auto/ethnographic accounts to be moral, and that the process of studying the self, gazing on the self within culture, should be a healing act. "Primarily written for sociological purposes, authors of personal narratives [in social sciences] often acknowledge a therapeutic side-effect to their work" (Elizabeth, 2008). Many auto/ethnographies deal with health issues—the breakdown of the body due to a number of diseases and illnesses (Penn, 2001; Rimmon-Kenan, 2002; Kolker, 1996); recovering and healing from the death of loved ones due to illness (Ellis, 1995, 1996, 2003; Lee, 2007) suicide (Lee, 2006); the loss of life from miscarriage or abortion (Ellis and Bochner, 2000). There are also auto/ethnographies of psychologists, doctors, and nurses who are emotionally entangled with the suffering of their patients (Riordan, 1996; Short, Grant and Clarke, 2007).

I would like to believe that this auto/ethnography has a moral base. Kelly made a promise to me to have the child— whether she made this promise due to my pressuring her or her fear that I was suicidal does not matter, because she should not have lied for those reasons. So the moral inquiry within personal and social relationship is: to what extent do we have an ethical responsibility when making a promise to another, especially a promise that has life altering effects and repercussions? To justify her lie, Kelly said, "Out of the seven sins, lying is the least." My response was, "You're also a murderer, because you promised Pabst his life and now you're taking it away from him," and proceeded to pontificate that her broken promise was a metaphorical murder, a symbolic act of abortion. The therapeutic component, for me, is the act of writing it down, getting it out of my system, and giving my emotions and pains the shape of a written personal narrative that, according to Ellis and Bochner (2000: 746),

> is part of the human, existential struggle to move life forward. [...] I get impatient with writers who belittle or diminish the therapeutic consequences of stories. They tend to draw a hard-and-fast distinction between therapy and social research, implying that narratives are useful only insofar as they advance sociological, anthropological or psychological theory. For these critics, narrative threatens the whole project of science [...] A text that functions as an agent of self-discovery or self-creation, for the author as well as for those who read and engage the text, is only threatening under a narrow definition of social inquiry, one that eschews a social science with a moral center and a heart. Why should caring and empathy be secondary to controlling and knowing? Why must academics be conditioned to believe that a text is important only to the extent it moves beyond the merely personal?

## AUTO/ANALYSIS

"The relationship story and writing about the relationship story occupied eighteen years of my life," writes Ellis (1995) in her account about losing a significant other to physical illness (a seminal text in the method of auto/ethnography). Similarly, it has taken me nearly two years to write this account; each time I have sat down to work on it, I have only been able to write for an hour. The emotions of loss come back, pain runs through my body, I begin to cry, am unable to think straight, and unable to write.

I reflect on how it came about that I have experienced such pain, how much of it is of my own agency and how much of it I can place the blame on Kelly or Nancy. The impetus for this experience was following the advice of a psychic; Nancy told me to reconnect with Kelly and have a relationship with her so the child would be born. Sociologists characterize the belief in psychics, parapsychology, metaphysics, and other matters similar as a "deviant behavior." Goode (2005: 259) categorizes belief in the paranormal and metaphysical as cognitive deviance: "deviant beliefs are identical in all basic respects to deviant acts [...] Someone, or a category of persons, is regarded by the members of one or more audiences as violating a rule or norm." Perhaps I am deviant; I know I do not adhere to mainstream thinking, and some people would consider whether or not I am insane having such beliefs. I also realize that since this paper is directed toward a social science audience, some may read this as a confession of a person who has psychological problems, that the visitations of the spirit I call Pabst are nothing more than visual and auditory hallucinations. I considered this as well, and previously noted that I thought he was made of my imagination, or a manifestation of my desire for something to become "real," not unlike Jung's contention that UFOs and aliens (another cognitive deviance) are visual manifestations for mankind's desire for space travel and hope that we are not alone in the vast universe.

In the threatening situation of the world today, when people are beginning to see that everything is at stake, the projection-creating fantasy soars beyond the realm of earthly organizations and powers into the heavens, into interstellar space, where the rulers of human fate, the gods, once had their abode in the planets [...]. Even people who would never have thought that a religious problem could be a serious matter that concerned them personally are beginning to ask themselves fundamental questions. Under these circumstances it would not be at all surprising if those sections of the community who ask themselves nothing were visited by "visions," by a widespread myth seriously believed in by some and rejected as absurd by others (Jung, 1979: 130).

In the end, what matters is what I believe, what is my reality; or as the symbolic interactionists say, what meaning I assign to things "by acting on things in terms of the meanings things have for them [...] Interactionists write about people who struggle to make sense of themselves and their life experiences" (Denzin, 1992: 25). Since Pabst had a certain meaning for me, proof that a child wanted to be born, I acted on this meaning by my interactions with Kelly to make this belief a shared reality between us.

The information I gave the researcher on a pain that never heals was a compact version of what I presented in this paper; the researcher was not looking for "thick description" that Denzin (2001: 31-33) identifies as interpretive interactionism when writing qualitative (auto) biographical texts:

Thick description attempts to uncover the means that inform and structure the subject's experience. It takes the reader to the heart of the experience that is being interpreted. It assumes that all meaning is symbolic and operates at the surface and the deep, and the micro and the macro levels. It turns on thick description, which always joins biography with lived experience.

Denzin derived from Mills (1959) an aegis of interpretive interaction, an evolutionary extension of symbolic interactionism (Blumer, 1969; Denzin, 1992). Denzin (2001: 99) contends interpretive interactionism

> seeks to bring lived experience before the reader. A major goal of the interpretive writer is to create a text that permits a willing reader to share vicariously in the experiences that have been captured. When this occurs, the reader can naturalistically generalize his or her experiences to those that have been captured [...] It is a form of performative writing. It creates verisimilitude, a space for the reader to imagine his or her way into the life experiences of another [...] [It] record[s] the voices of lived experience, or the "prose of the world."

At issue here is interpersonal communication and the misunderstanding of communication in personal relationships through

> a text that permits a willing reader to share vicariously the experiences that have been captured. When this happens, the reader can naturally generalize (Stake, 1978, p. 5) his or her experiences to those that can been captured" (Denzin, 2001: 87).

The need to procreate is an issue that falls under the ideas put forth by Mills (1959) in *The Sociological Imagination*. Mills posits that the personal problems of individuals reflect the problems of society at large, and both are interconnected and entwined. In this case, my desire to experience fatherhood in my late 30s, closing in on middle-age, is a social issue that many men are experiencing today; careers, failed relationships and marriages, economic and political climates are obstacles to starting a family. People in general seem to be starting their families later in life than they did fifty, a hundred years ago. As men become older, their pool of companions for possible wives and mothers diminish as women in their same age range (late 30s-late 40s) can no longer (for health reasons) have children; or the women in the man's social circle are married and unavailable, or divorced/single, already have children and do not wish for more. Thus, men feeling and "hearing the biological clock ticking" must seek out women younger than they are, which can meet with mixed social and personal results. Another issue is the inability for some men and women to effectively communicate, within a variety of relationships (romantic, friends, marriage, business) exactly what it is they want from the other, and what they want together, to fulfill a personal need or desire. When this communication is dysfunctional, misunderstanding results in pain, sadness, and anger. These are the issues I had to deal with when the desire to be a father overtook my thoughts and emotions, yet none of the women I was meeting were suitable or willing candidates.

This auto/ethnography also questions the validity of my memory. Am I recalling events correctly? Memory is subjective, and we add and subtract moments, dialogue, interaction, intentions, and interpretation of conversations in relationships to best suit the way we prefer to remember the past and how we fashion personal reality (Gubrian, 1988). We tell and write stories to organize our reality and make sense of our lives (Riessman, 1993); the terminology for the social practice is articulation (Gubrian, 1988) and ethnomethodology (Garfinkel, 1967) that "pertains to practical methods of reasoning used by people to sort and assign meaning to experience" (Gubrian, 1988: 22). Using this process of the layered account (Ronai, 1992, 1996), I create a narrative to make sense of what caused the pain, inside me, that will never heal. It was my intention that this paper was be therapeutic; however, (auto)writing as therapy is supposed to help the process of healing…and I am never going to heal from the death of an idea: the loss of my son's life. I will admit that my representations in this paper are subjective to my beliefs and desires; I have left out many moments and conversations that are not overall relevant (and would make this paper book-length, albeit a boring volume) and have "collapsed" certain events (Ellis, 2004: 126).

Kelly's memories of these events will differ from mine, and are just as biased. Her assignment of meanings differ from mine—for instance, a friend of hers said I wanted her to have a baby to trap her into a relationship, so she would not be with someone else. Kelly considered this and I said that was not true. She also thought I wanted to use her body as a "vessel" for my (our) son, that I was not considering her feelings and well-being. She said I pressured her, guilt-tripped her about the abortions, was only seeing the world in "black and white."

## AUTO/BIOLOGY: A CONCLUSION

This essay has been an account of a biological need transformed into a psychological and spiritual desire and how I acted on my needs and desires. Biologically, we are designed with the drive to procreate, even against logical odds-- Neville-Jan (2004) writes of having a baby no matter how much health risk it puts her in; it is after all natural if the human race is to continue. Ellis (1991), Lincoln and Denzin (2003) call for auto/ethnography to be moral stories that are healing and cause transformation, but the transformation I have experienced, that I have written about, is that the pain and loss of my desire has only left me a broken man (adding to it the death of Trudi). I am still in grieving, the way any parent never gets over the death of a child. There has been no healing. This experience is indeed a pain that will never go away, a hole in my heart that will never close up, to return to the research question at the top of this paper. I am condemned to live with it every day because I am doomed to remember the way things "could have been," and I am convinced, as is the case with all memory and reflection, that if events had worked out, and the child were alive, and Kelly and I had different lives as parents, our lives would be better than they are now. There would not be the anger, distrust, and betrayal that now exists between us, separating us.

That presence, that spirit, that dancing blue ribbon I called Pabst, that idea of a life, that dream of a child—he does not come around as much as he used to. Sometimes he does, and I can feel him next to me, in the room with me, and sometimes I see him. I wish I could say that I am pleased to have him visit; the truth is, his presence only hurts, and I break down and cannot function, because I re-experience grief once more. Perhaps that is why he does not show himself like he used to, so I won't have to be in pain. Does he visit Kelly too? I would like to think that he does. Whether or not she is aware of him, and thinks of him, and wonders how life would have been like had she not broken her promises to Heaven, I will never know.

The last time he came to me in a dream, I woke up and wrote on a piece of paper:

Somewhere,
an infant glanced up
and saw a small angel
unfolding wings.

A poet once said
of such joys:
"How the spirit rose,
as a dove.
I called 'my child'
while waters
and air splashed all around."

I believe we were all
that young where the open skies,
a laughing face, a bird, a child,
an angel
or just someone else
was as easy as the sun behind leaves –

rim of light,
semi-circle halo on our fingertips.

When I wonder and worry,
I try to remember this.

I see the face of the child:
it has become old and faded.

## Note

1.  I am indebted to Art Bocher for his helpful comments about this
    section when he reviewed this essay as a submission to a journal. I
    could only be so lucky as to have been a student of his.

# References

Behar, R. (1996) *The vulnerable observer: Anthropology that breaks your heart.* Boston: Basic Books.

Cohen, Anthony P. (1994). *Self-consciousness: An alternative anthropology of identity.* New York: Routledge.

Denzin, N.K. (1992). *Symbolic interactionism and cultural studies.* Oxford: Blackwell.

Denzin, N.K. (1997). *Interpretive ethnography: Ethnographic practices for the 21st century.* Thousand Oaks, CA: Sage.

Denzin, N.K. (2001). *Interpretive interactionism.* 2nd ed. Applied Social Research Methods Series 16. Thousand Oaks: Sage.

Denzin, N.K. and Lincoln, Y. (2003). *Collecting and interpreting qualitative materials.* Thousand Oaks: Sage.

DeSalvo, L. (1999). *Writing as a way of healing: How telling our stories transforms ourlives.* Boston: Beacon Press.

Elizabeth, V. (2007). Another string to our bow: Participant writing as research method *Forum Qualitative Sozialforschung / Forum: Qualitative Social Research,* 9(1). http://www.qualitative-research.net/fqs-texte/1-08/08-1-31-e.htm.

Ellis, C. (1991). *Sociological introspection and emotion experience.* Symbolic interaction, 14, 23-50.

Ellis, C. (1995). *Final negotiations: a story of love, loss, and chronic illness.* Philadelphia: Temple University Press.

71

Ellis, C. (2003a). Maternal connections. In Ellis C. and Bochner, A.P. (eds), *Composing ethnography: Alternative forms of qualitative writing.* Walnut Creek: AltaMira Press.

Ellis, C. (1997). Evocative autoethnography: Writing emotionally about our lives. In William Tierney & Yvonna Lincoln (Eds.), *Representation and the text* (pp.115-139). New York: SUNY Press.

Ellis, C. (1998). I hate my voice: Coming to terms with minor bodily stigmas. *The Sociological Quarterly, 39*(4), 517-537.

Ellis, C. (1999). Heartful autoethnography. *Qualitative Health Research, 9*(5), 669-683.

Ellis, Carolyn (2003b). Grave tending: With Mom at the cemetery. *Forum Qualitative Sozialforschung / Forum: Qualitative Social Research,* 4(2), http://www.qualitativeresearch. net/fqs-texte/2-03/2-03ellis-e.htm
Ellis, C. (2004). *The ethnographic I.* Walnut Creek: AltaMira Press.

Ellis, C., & Bochner, A. (2000). Autoethnography, personal narrative, reflexivity: researcher as subject. In N. K. Denzin & Y. S. Lincoln (Eds.), *Handbook of qualitative research* (2nd ed., pp. 733-768). Thousand Oaks: Sage.

Esgalhado, B. M. D. (2002). For then and now: Memory and writing. *Narrative Inquiry, 11*(2), 235-256.

Garfinkel, H. (1969). *Studies in ethnomethodology.* Englewood: Prentice-Hall.

Geertz, C. (1998). *Work and lives: The Anthropologist as author.* Cambridge: UK polity.

Goode, E. (1995) *Deviant behavior* (7th ed). Upper Saddle River, NJ: Pearson.

Gubrian, J.(1988). *Analyzing field reality.* Newbury Park: Sage.

Hallett, E. and Carmen, N. (2000). *Cosmic cradle.* Fairfield, IA: Sumtar Publishing.

Hallett, E. (2002a). *Hearing the soul's voice: a mid-wife's tale.* URL: http://www.birthpsychology.com/lifebefore/concept15.html

Hallett, E. (2002b). *Stories of the unborn soul: The mystery and delight of pre-birth communication* NY: iUniverse.

Hallett, E. (1995). *Soul trek: Meeting our children on the way to birth.* Hamilton, MT: Light Hearts Publishing.

Hemmingson, M., ed. (2001a). *The mammoth book of legal thrillers.* NY: Carroll & Graf.

Hemmingson, M. (2001b). *Wild turkey.* NY: Forge.

Hemmingson, M. (2004). *The rose of heaven.* Halicog, PA: Prime Books.

Hemmingson, M. Milk. (2007). In *Art of the one act.* Kalamazoo, MI: New Issues Press.

Holt, N. L. (2003). Representation, legitimation, and autoethnogr phy: an autoethnographic writing story. *International Journal of Qualitative Methods,* 2(1). http://www.ualberta.ca/~iiqm/backissues/2_1/html/holt.html

Jung, C.G. (1979). *Flying saucers: a modern myth of things seen in the skies.* Princeton: Princeton University Press.

Kehily, M.J. (1995). Self-narration, autobiography and identity construction. *Gender and Education,* 7(1), 23-31.

Lee, K.V. (2006) A fugue about grief. *QualitativeInquiry,* 12(6), 1154-1159.
Lee, K.V. (2007) Georgie's girl: Last conversations with my father. *Journal of social work practice* 21(3), 289-296.

Lincoln, Y.S. & Denzin, N.K. (2003). *Turning Points in Qualitative Research: Tying Knots in a Handkerchief.* Walnut Creek, CA: Alta Mira Press.

Mills, C.W. (1959). *The sociological imagination*. New York: Oxford University Press.

Moss, R. *Dreaming true*. (2000). NY: Pocket Books.

Neville-Jan, A. (2004). Selling your soul to the devil: an autoethngraphy of paim, pleasure, and The quest for a child. *Disability & Society 19* (2), 113-127.

Payne, D. Autobiology. (1996). In Ellis C. and Bochner, A.P. (eds) *Composing ethnography: Alternative forms of qualitative writing*. Walnut Creek: AltaMira Press.

Penn, P, (2001). Chronic illness: Trauma, language and writing: Breaking the silence. *Family Process, 40*(1), 33-52.

Pennebaker, J. (1990). *Opening up: The healing power of expressing emotions*. New York: Guilford Press.

Thompson, K. (2004). Journal writing as a therapeutic tool. In Gillie Bolton, Stephanie Howlett, Colin Lago & Jeannie K. Wright (Eds.). *Writing cures: An introductory handbook of writing in counselling and therapy* (pp.72-84). Hove & New York: Brunner Routledge.

Richardson, L. (2001). Getting personal: Writing stories. *Qualitative Studies in Education, 14*(1), 33-38.

Richardson, L. (2002). Writing sociology. *Cultural Studies—Critical Methodologies, 2*(3), 414-422.

Riessman, C.K. *Narrative analysis*. (1993). Newbury Park: Sage.

Rimmon-Kenan, S. The story of "I": Illness and narrative identity. *Narrative 10*(1): 9-27.

Riordan, Richard J. (1996). Scriptotherapy: Therapeutic writing as a counseling adjunct. *Journal of Counseling & Development, 74*, 263-269.

Rose, N. (1990). *Governing the soul: The shaping of the private self.* London: Routledge.

Short, N.P., Grant, A. and Clarke, K. (2007). Living in the borderland; writing in the margins: an autoethnographic tale. *Journal of psychiatric and mental health nursing,* 14, 771-782.

Stanley, L. (1993). On auto/biography in sociology. *Sociology,* 27(1), 41-52.

Tom, A. and Herbert, C. P. (2002). The "near miss": A story of relationship. *Qualitative Inquiry, 8*(5), 591-607.

Vickers, Margaret H. (2002). Researchers as storytellers: Writing on the edge—and without a safety net. *Qualitative Inquiry, 8*(5), 608-621.

# AUTO/ETHNOGRAPHY IN TWO POEMS

In the mid-1990s, I was employed by an international wire service as a foreign correspondent. I was assigned to hot spots around the world because I wanted to be there, I wanted to witness and experience strife and danger. I did this because I was under the youthful impression that this is what writers *did*, for future books—memoir, the novel, maybe a film. Worked for Hemingway, right? And it worked for William T. Vollmann, which is why I wound up co-editing *Expelled from Eden* (2004), a "reader" of his collected works.

I attempted to write about my experiences in Rwanda many times, without success. I tried the short story, the essay, the play—none seemed to work. The play, *Bosnia*, was 90 minutes long—a three-character piece about a war correspondent dealing with the woman he loved, and her dealing with his constantly going off to war zones and never knowing if he'll come back. The female in the play was a composite of many woman I had relationships with while I was a journalist—none of them waited for me to come back home, they could not deal with being in a serious relationship with a man who might return in a body bag. The play had a limited run at the small theater company I was literary manager of, The Fritz in San Diego, and received lukewarm reviews and audience reception. The full frontal nudity seemed to be the greatest draw for theater-goers in a city that is not theater-friendly.

I took the text of the play and made it a section in my erotic novel, *The Comfort of Women* (2001). My editor had me remove the section—he didn't feel the mixture of war and death and explicit sexual content worked well for a commercial mass-market paperback. I thought it worked perfectly. "Keep that section for another book someday," he said. The parent company of the erotic imprint was Thunder's Mouth Press, a reputable literary house that published Nation Books and many political titles. My editor told me if I put together a comprehensive proposal about my experiences in Rwanda, or other countries such as Bosnia and Somalia where I had been sent to, he would give me a contract and decent advance.

I tried, for several months, to get the memoir together, but I could not—not in a way that I thought would effectively, honestly tell my life narrative the way I felt it should. I would purposely leave matters out, events or experiences I didn't wish to recall in writing, or added in dialogue and situations that as fictional, just to make the text read more interesting (for there were many dull days). Neither worked. Perhaps I needed more time and distance.

This seemed to be true with others-ten years after the genocide in Rwanda, narrative representations stated to come out, from novels to biographies to memoirs, studies, and a film, *Hotel Rwanda* (which I have been unable to watch without breaking down in tears and turning it off).

Someday I will be able to sit down and write about what I saw, felt, experienced, and processed. For now, I have this poem. It does the job in few words—and maybe that is all that truly needs to be said. When I have read it in front of an audience, someone always comes up to me and asks, "Is that true or fiction?" It never occurred to me that fiction was employed in the poetic form—culturally, it has been imbedded in belief system that poetry equates memoir, truth. Perhaps I have read too many confessional poets, such as Charles Bukowski, Sharon Olds, and Jack Gilbert. But were not Shakespeare's sonnets written for, and about, real people in his life? Emily Dickenson, Walt Whitman, Allen Ginsberg—they all wrote about their lives, about real people, real events, real feelings. I did not take into account Shel Silverstein or Dr. Suess. "But even autobiographical poetry does not merely recount the poet's life," writes Blue (2001).

> Those details will be redrawn and reshaped wherever necessary to fulfill the aesthetic and thematic demands of the poem.
>
> If the actual details of the life are incompatible with the requirements of the poem, the poem's needs will inevitably take precedence over mere truth, sometimes without the poet's even being aware that he is reshaping truth in the image of art.
>
> Furthermore, "truth" and "memory" are surprisingly flexible for most people. No matter how honest the poet, no matter how determined to present what actually happened, he is bound--as we all are--to offer instead a fictionalized version of events.

When people ask me that question, I say, "As best as I can recall, yes, it is true."

*September 11, 2007*: There was plenty of reflection and commentary to choose from on the television and radio. On MSNBC, all day long the cable channel replayed archived news coverage and footage, from the very beginning when it was speculated that a plane had accidentally hit the World

Trade Center, to when the towers fell and images of soot and dust-covered people were broadcast across the globe. I picked up Don DeLillo's *Falling Man* and began reading. The novel concerns that day and the week after in the lives of three people, with flashbacks of Mohammed Atta and a few other jihadists living in Germany, getting ready to go the United States and enroll in flight schools. Six years later, it seems the right time for DeLillo to comment on the experience in fictional form. There has been an onslaught of 9/11 novels appearing since 2005, from first books to works by proclaimed contemporary masters of prose. Cyberpunk writer William Gibson's *Pattern Recognition* is set in the near-future and touches on 9/11, as a woman who works in the intelligence community starts to realize that her father, a CIA agent who supposedly died in the World Trade Center a decade ago, may have used the incident as an excuse to disappear and go underground, living somewhere under a new name and identity. "The debut of these fictional accounts...years after that horribly memorable day -- may be one indication of America's readiness to see the tragedy through a different lens," contends Owuor (2005).

> Historically, artists have felt compelled to paint, dramatize, and write about events of their day -- and often, their work transcends their own generation and becomes an artistic benchmark of a historical event....As 9/11 becomes more distant, broaching the subject in a less literal way may be timely and appropriate for healing grief, some say.
>
> Mental-health experts who have dealt with those directly affected by 9/11 give conflicting views about the ability of fictional accounts of that day to help people recover from grief.

This is true in my own experience, writing about 9/11. Days after that day, I composed a poems, "Falling," presented alongside "Rwanda.". It is auto/ethnography about my thoughts and feelings on that day, and reactions to the images I witnessed on the television set.

I sent "Falling" out to numerous magazines and journals and didn't have any success in getting it published. "Falling" didn't garner negativity; editors replied that it was too long and one, at *The New Yorker*, scribbled on the rejection slip: "It's too soon for this." My one published 9/11 text, a story, "Tuck," was published in an anthology and reprinted in Japan, Germany, and Italy; it was complete fiction, about people I didn't know and experiences I never had. Fiction, rather than autobiography, was an acceptable way for me to create cultural commentary.

Today, when I read "Falling" in front of audiences, my approach in context being performance ethnography, the reaction received is positive; people nod in approval and tell me, later, the poem reminds them of where they were and what they were experiencing on the day in question. I do not, however, read the Atta poem, for many reasons.

# RWANDA

## JULY-AUGUST, 1994

**1.**

Rows of bodies.
As we drove to the border at Goma, Zaire,
it looked like the bodies extended for miles.

Covered in abandoned cloth or makeshift mats,
or not covered at all,
the dead were lined alongside the road
as if they were awaiting turns
into the passage of nowhere,
and *nowhere* was where we were;
age, sex, clothing didn't differentiate,
they were from every class,
from the poor who were always poor
to the the elite now running away
and living among the impecunious.
I saw an albino black child dead
among the populace of the dead.
Other small children stood alone,
crying and confused,
looking around for lost parents or siblings.
There was another line, that of the living,
the migration that had begun,
the search for safety in a neighboring nation,
the fear of the future behind them like a stalker in a city street.

### 2.

It wasn't easy sleeping
in the Red Cross tents.
I kept hearing children
crying, adults crying,
people shouting,
a few scattered gun shots
now and then
deep in Zaire.
And it was hot, of course.

The mosquitoes were out,
flying about the bodies, swarming over the lake and river
where there were more bodies.

### 3.

I took five showers that first day
back in America.
I couldn't get the stench of
all those bodies off me.
There were bodies dancing in my head,
and I wanted to dance with them.

### 4.

I was acting strangely and
people were telling me so.
On the one hand, I wasn't
talking about Rwanda.
People sent me e-mail,
called me, asked me,
"So what was it like?"
I was very minimal in response.
"It was hot, smelly,
and disgusting," said I,
and I said no more.
Maybe they thought
I would come back morose,
with decrepit tales
in the apocalyptic language
of the slaughterhouse.
But I was cracking jokes,
sending people strange e-mail,

and drinking.
                    I was drinking and not sleeping.
Well, I'd get in a few hours of sleep.
I'd wake up and start drinking at eight, nine a.m.
I called people on the phone, people all over,
to talk about anything, anything but Rwanda.
I had bags under my eyes.
I wanted to go out and party,
to dance, to raise hell.
Those dead bodies were dancing in my head
and I wanted to slam dance with them all, the fuckers.


### 5.
Something wasn't right.


### 6.
The next week, I calmed down.
I was feeling better.
I could sort this out now.
I went down to the  beach in La Jolla
and listened to the waves crash to the shore.
I waded in the water.
I think I saw what looked like a sting ray— or maybe
that was a jellyfish—in the water.
The news that morning said
something about being careful,
the heat was bringing them closer
into shore.  I didn't care.
I liked the feel of the ocean
splashing on me,

salt taste in my mouth,
and not the taste of death—
death on my tongue,
on the roof of my mouth
like some kind of evil jam.

### 7.

For a moment, I felt a strange and
soothing calmness, like everything would be all right,
and it would be all right
for the rest of my life.
The waves pulled away,
went back to the sea,.
That feeling was only for a moment.

# FALLING

*It is either the beginning or the end
of the world, and the choice is ourselves
or nothing.*
                    —*Carolyn Forché*

### 1.

I sleep with
the radio on, listening to Art Bell
which always makes for interesting dreams.
That morning, I was having one
about hijacked planes and I awoke,

hearing a man's voice on the radio
announce that a second jet
had smashed into the World Trade Center
like leviathans clashing in
a Japanese monster movie.
I thought: What the hell has
been going on in the world
while I was asleep?
When I turned the TV
on to CNN—always CNN—
the twin towers had already
collapsed. I thought I was
still asleep.  No, I was like
Lazarus beseeched from the grave,
afraid. Confused.


## 2.

Dominique—
I told you, back in 1991,
that a day like this would come,
when the United States would be
invaded or attacked; I told you this
during the days and nights
of Desert Storm. I watched
*that* war on TV, alone in
my small apartment,
when you went back to Paris
for Christmas.
You called one night
and said you were scared,
your voice distant and

digital, overseas.

When the news of the
World Trade Center reached
you in France, did you
think of me? Did you wonder
if I was safe? Did you try
and find my number,
my email, from estranged
mutual friends?
You should know I have
been to Africa since, and
I am not the same.

### 3.

News and multiple channels
filled my head with
the pornography of
this violence.
I can't sleep.
I don't want to sleep.
I want to watch,
I want the latest breaking news.
I'm like an excited crowd member
in a public arena, waiting
for the condemned to hang,
to face Dr. Guillotine's blade,
to stand before the
firing squad or ravished lions.

### 4.

Karin—

so, two weeks after moving
to New York,
you had death stop by
for breakfast.
You went to the city
looking for a new life
with that new husband of yours.
I hope you're happy—no,
that is a lie.
I hope you're safe,
and that is the truth.


### 5.

The TV was lying to me.
I heard different things
from people I knew
in New York—the emails,
the phone calls, the postcards.
    *We've all put ourselves into the*
*lives of the victims, the heroes —*
someone said this on TV,
a politician, a commentator.
I looked at the aftermath
and knew the smell
was bad; death like
the air at the edge of
the Salton Sea in California.
The TV didn't like to talk much
about the smell of death.
I know the scent—I remember it well
when I was in Rwanda,
1994, the rows and rows

of bodies, miles of the dead.
Water killed them.
Cholera.

### 6.

Yes, I have put myself
into their lives.
I'm one of the heroes
rushing the hijackers
on Flight 93
like a fallen angel
living in the hour far
from Allah. I'm also
one of the New York Firemen
trapped and killed
and then buried in the rubble.
I am the falling "debris."
I am one of the flight
crew, hands tied,
necks slit open,
dead.

### 7.

The image that haunts me most
is the footage of the man and woman
who held hands as they jumped
from the burning World Trade Center.
I am both of them
making that final choice.
I would've leapt, had I been there.
I would've fallen

and falling, news cameras would've
filmed it,
and people would've decried sounds
of wonder and horror—the spectacle!
I would've been on CNN or Fox News.
I'm sure time would've stood
still as I made my way down;
the world
would've engulfed me,
warmed me,
and given me a nice fluffy
pillow so I could finally sleep,
and sleeping,
I would've dreamed;
I would wake up to a different
life on a different earth
where God still had many names
and just one face.

## References

Blue, T. (2001). Why an autobiographical poem is *not* autobiography..
Retrieved September 30, 2008 at
http://tinablue.homestead.com/becky3.html

DeLillo, D. *Falling man*. (2007). NY: Scribner.

Denzin, N.K. (2003). *9/11 in american culture*. Walnut Creek: AtaMira.

Denzin, N.K.. (2003). *Performance ethnography: critical pedagogy and the politics of culture*. Thousand Oaks: Sage.

George, T., director. (2004). *Hotel Rwanda*. United Artists Films.

Gibson, W. *Pattern recognition*. (2003). NY: Putnam.

Hemmingson, M. *The comfort of women*. (2001). NY: Blue Moon Books.

Hemmingson, M. Tuck. In Mamatas, N., editor. (2004). *Urban bizarre*. Halicog, PA: Prime Books.

Madison, D.S. (2005). *Critical ethnography: method, ethics, and performance*. Thousand Oaks: Sage.

Owuor, E. (2005). Fiction with 9/11 themes begins to fill U.S. bookstores. *The Christian Science Monitor*, 19 April.

# TIJUANA AND TRAMADOL

## BORDER REFLECTIONS ON ADDICTION TO AN OVER-THE-COUNTER DRUG

I became hooked on a certain pharmaceutical purchased over-the-counter in Tijuana called Tramadol. It was the last thing I expected: becoming, for want of a better, sugarcoated term, *a junkie*. I was addicted and did not know how this happened. It was certainly never my intention and I did not think it could be possible. These things just creep on you and then you are trapped in your need and you do not know what to do, you do not know where to turn, except inside: where you re-examine your life and find out where it all began, and try to come up with a means of bringing it to an end, short of checking into rehab like a celebutante after a series of scandals and bad press.

Tramadol is a synthetic, centrally acting analgesic that was approved for use in Australia in 1998 (Lebate, 2005). It is an atypical opioid which is a centrally acting analgesic, used for treating moderate to severe pain. It is a synthetic agent, as a 4-phenyl-piperidine analogue of Codeine, and appears to have actions on the Gabaergic, noradrenergic and serotonergic systems. Tramadol was developed by the German pharmaceutical company Grünenthal GmbH and marketed under the trade name Tramal. Grünenthal has also cross-licensed the drug to many other pharmaceutical companies that market it under various names like Ultram, Ultracet, and Tramacet. Dosages vary depending on the degree of pain experienced by the patient.

When I initially checked Drugs.com, my understanding concluded Tramadol was not habit-forming; it wasn't narcotics-based like Vicodin or Oxycotin. The first bottle I purchased was manufactured from a Mexican company called Venadrol; the bottle contained fifty pills and cost $18 at a pharmacy on Third and Revolución, next to the Burger King. I had walked in to procure Metaformin, a drug for those with Type II diabetes that assists the pancreas in correctly processing sugar into the bloodstream. In Tijuana, Metaformin was $10 for a bottle of 100, compared to a $25 co-pay at Keiser Permanente, $60 without insurance.

I asked the pharmacist if they had Vicodin. He shook his head and said, "Not without a prescription." I thought a prescription wasn't needed—this was *Tijuana*, after all, and street barkers sold Vicodin and Oxycotin for $5-10 a pill, along with meth, coke, and ecstasy.[1]

"We have muscle relaxants," the pharmacist told me. "If you need a pain stopper, these do the same job."

"Yeah?"

"Take two or three, it is like one Vicodin," he said.

Sold.

*Vicodin.* Kelly had strained her neck and was prescribed Vicodin. I asked her what the drug was like. She said, "You should try it, it's fun." All I could think of was the Eminem rap song where he raps about mixing booze and Vicodin and going homicidal with a chainsaw. One weekend, Liv took two pills and gave me one. Within half an hour, I was feeling the effect: as if I were partially underwater. A warmth spread throughout my body, slowly, like spilt syrup on linoleum; my head felt light and airy and my brain was a feather in the breeze.

"What do you think?" Kelly asked.

"Not bad."

"Want another?"

I nodded in the affirmative.

She gave me another.

"How many can you take before it's dangerous?" I asked.

"Two should be the limit, these are 100 milligrams." She then told me about how, a couple years ago when she was a cocktail waitress, she had serious migraines and was given Vicodin by her doctor. She had to take three at work to function. "Three can tranq out a horse," she said, "I couldn't even feel my feet. How did I walk? I was gliding, floating. But I got through my shift, that's all that mattered."[2]

I would occasionally ask Kelly for two or three Vicodins when she had them, by way of one of her doctors. "All you want to do is get high," she'd accuse, but that wasn't the case: they didn't really get me high and I didn't care about getting high. What the pharmaceutical did was put me in a curious lucid dream state; I would lie in bed or on the couch and go into a zone where I was not quite asleep, but not conscious either. I was convinced that, inside my head, the squishy matter called my noggin was capable of traveling forward and backward through time and space. I could re-examine, in detail, certain memories; I could peer into days yet to come and see what my future would consist of. I could also piece together scenes and dialogue for novels and screenplays.

I was writing several screenplays at the time. I was beginning my pursuit for Hollywood; just like the Vicodin, Kelly was to blame. On Valentine's Day, she said instead of tossing darts at pictures of all her ex-boyfriends, she wanted to get drunk. We had dinner at a German restaurant in Ocean Beach, drank plenty of German beer. Tipsy, she became melancholy and remorseful. She started to cry. I held her. She talked about regrets and how hard it was to be a single mother. "Look what my life is because I happened to screw the wrong guy." She didn't blame her daughter; she loved that child and knew it was right to have her instead of getting an abortion. The custody agreement with the father, however, didn't allow her to take the kid out of San Diego. "I'm stuck here," Liv said, "I'm trapped in my life." She was a theater actress but didn't have time to do more than one or two shows a year, because she had to work and tend to the needs of her family; and because she couldn't move from San Diego with her daughter, she couldn't explore a life in Los Angeles as an actress.

I asked: "What is it that you really, truly want? Tell me, and I'll get it for you."

She said: "To be an actress in independent films."

"I can do that," I said. My professional writing career included many published novels, stories, articles and plays; while I'd optioned a couple of my books that were never fully developed, I never sat down to write screenplays. I knew that I would write them, eventually, and *now* seemed the right time. "I'll write screenplays for us both to do," I said, "we'll produce them low budget and get Hollywood's attention, and we'll be filmmakers."

It happens all the time, right?

"What I need right now is a Vicodin," she said. "Want one?"

"How about two?"

I wrote a couple of character-driven dramas and a thriller, but I knew I had to create scripts that were "high concept," as they say in Tinsel Town: ultra-commercial, movies that the masses would happily pay $9 to see. That meant romantic comedies, family comedies, and teen sex comedies: movies I didn't pay money to go see, genres I didn't enjoy writing. On Vicodin, however, I seemed to get sentimental and shallow, and found myself creating silly romantic comedies. "This is so *unlike* you," Liv said, "this is so—*commercial!*"

So whenever I asked for Vicodins from her, and she protested that I was depleting her stash, I'd say, "I can't finish that romantic comedy! I can only write like that on the pills. I have to finish this project, it's important, so we can go to Hollywood."

In light of that logic, she gave in. (I should note that two of those sappy screenplays have been optioned by producers, but not in Hollywood: one in New York and one in San Diego.)

The supply of Vicodin ended when our friendship went south.

I traveled south to write a series of articles (for an alternative weekly) about the Tijuana police and the state of safety for American tourists. *El jefe* of the biggest drug cartel in Baja had been apprehended by the FBI while holed up inside the

Dolphin Motel, and now there was a battle going on between several cartels for control of Tijuana. Some police officers were targeted for assassination, and when the bullets started to fly, bystanders were getting hit in the crossfire. Some of them were American tourists. Tourism started to drastically drop after that. My first trip down there, five cops rousted me on First and Revolución; they stole $60 from my pocket. A month later, the Federales took their guns away, to test which pistols may have been used in homicides, so there was no police presence anywhere. There were plenty of Federales, though, with machine guns mounted to the roof of their vehicles; there was also the Mexican army, traveling on troop transports and in tanks through the city street. I started to wonder if I was in Baghdad or Tijuana. The tourist areas were bleak—like a ghost town. Vendors were hurting for money. I couldn't walk one block without being hounded by barkers trying to get me into their stores and clubs. When the Taco Bell has a barker outside, urging you to come in and buy a *gordita*, that's a sign that things are dire.

I was taking two or three pills of Tramadol a day; at first they put me in that lucid dream state like Vicodin, but I had to up the dosage as my tolerance level increased. I was then at seven pills a day, 50 milligrams each.

I had just turned forty and my body was beginning to betray me with the gradual increase of little aches and pains in the joints, in my lower back. The Tramadol made those go away. I was sleeping less, as the drug was a bit of an upper, so I was getting more writing done. How could this be bad? I had no pain and I was productive.

When the pills ran out, the trouble arrived. I didn't have any plans on getting more; I would get the stuff whenever I had a reason for going across the border. Two days with no pills, the aches and pains returned, only they seemed three times worse than before. I was also sleeping ten-twelve a stretch, catching up on what I'd lost; awake, I was groggy, cranky, and uncomfortable.

I made a special trip to TJ just to get "my medicine," as I told my friends.

I was taking 10-15 pills per day by now.

It was not a narcotic, it was not illegal (although I never declared the bottle in my pocket to the Customs agent when crossing back into the U.S.), I was not getting high—I was merely dulling the physical pain, the same way anyone uses aspirin or IB Profin. This was my justification.

I continued this routine for three months: every ten days I would get on the trolley and enter Mexico like a Cold War secret agent sneaking past the Berlin Wall, on a mission. I'd walk into the first pharmacy past the gates (there are three next to the McDonald's), pay $35 for a bottle of 100 pills, get a couple of tasty tacos from sidewalk vendors (the finest tacos in the world are from the streets of Tijuana), and cross back. I figured out the best times to avoid long lines at the border: early morning or after 8 p.m. Between noon and 7 p.m., tourists and commuters head back to the states, and you could find yourself standing in line forty, fifty minutes, even an hour and a half.

This was turning into an expensive habit: $140 a month. I decided to stop. I could deal with the minor leg and back discomforts.

The first day was bearable. On the second, I experienced hot and cold flashes running through my body, as if I had the flu. My skin itched, my legs twitched. Jolts of pain ran up and down my spine. I couldn't sleep and I was sweating, whether I was hot or cold or in between. I took some over-the-counter sleeping pills and they had no effect. I took more. I drank eight beers. I still couldn't sleep. I was exhausted, staring at the TV for hours, dumbfounded by my condition, watching late night *Star Trek* and cable news/infotainment. Finally, I did sleep for about five hours, and when I woke up, I was drenched in sweat and shivering.

My body was stiff like a new corpse.

I could barely stand up.

I knew what William Burroughs must have felt like, or Jim Carroll in *The Basketball Diaries*—I ran down a list of distinguished literary junkies and decided the footsteps I was treading in weren't that bad.

"Guess what," I told friends on the phone and in emails, "I'm a junkie."

None of them found it as amusing as I. How did this happen? How did I sink this low? I always thought of myself beyond that, stronger than this; that I would never succumb to being dependent on chemicals like some kind of...some kind of *William Burroughs character.*

I was angry with myself. "Stupid stupid stupid."

I conducted in-depth research on the Internet about Tramadol, all the while in lofty misery and anguish. I read about people dying from it; I read about mental and sexual side effects. One could go bipolar and have sex like a Tantric love god...

I thought about my life and everything I didn't have—children, a wife, a home I owned—and wept like a new widower. I read that Tramadol was like anti-depressants; this explained the overwhelming feeling of doom. I was postpartum in my mind.

I could not take any more. I could not face another sleepless night, praying to God to make it all go away. I hopped on the trolley and headed for the border, *La Línea*, TJ.

My legs were so stiff that it took me fifteen minutes to walk across the bridge, when it usually took five. I kept thinking, "Almost there, almost there" like The Little Train That Could, trekking up the mountain.

At the gates to my salvation, five barkers in white pharmacist jackets from all three *farmacías* beseeched me to come into their havens of pleasure.

*"Right here, amigo!"*

*"Pasole, Mister!"*

*"I have what you need, broheim!"*

How did they know what I required? Was it that obvious? I imagined myself looking like a starving zombie in need of a large lunch plate made of fresh, gooey brains.

"One bottle of Citra 50," I said. Citra was a manufacturer that had a special on bottles of 100, with 25 extra *gratis.*

"Tramadol?" asked the pharmacist.

"That's the ticket, amigo."

"Only one bottle? How about three?"

My body was shaking. I thought my knees were going to give out. I pleaded: *"Just get me the one bottle, por favor."*

I also grabbed a Fanta orange soda from the fridge. I paid $35.75 for both items. Bottle in hand, I quickly opened it, broke the seal, cracked open the soda, put the bottle to my mouth, let four or five pills fall on my tongue like Heaven rejecting rebellious seraphim, and washed them down with the soda.

My eyes were closed the whole time.

I sighed, loudly. I was safe.

I opened my eyes—two pharmacists were staring at me. Yes, me: the hapless, hopeless pain pill junkie gringo.

"Are you okay, my friend?"

"I am now."

I was ashamed. Ashamed on many levels. I turned around and couldn't get to U.S. soil fast enough.

I hated Tijuana. I hated everything about it and I vowed never to set foot in this vile city again.

I was ashamed but kept taking the pills. I loathed TJ but returned twice, going to a different pharmacy each trip. Soon, my abhorrence turned into love; I was getting addicted to the sights, smells, and sounds of the city because I related it to my drug.

There was no way I was going to be able to go cold turkey; my body couldn't take it and I didn't have the leisure to be out of commission for a week or two. I would have to slowly, gradually, wean myself off this hideous indigence.

It took five weeks. I went from ten-to-fifteen pills a day to seven-to-ten. Then seven. Then six. And five. I quietly celebrated the day I could get by with taking two.

One morning I woke up and felt fine and knew I didn't need a single pill. I took what was left in the bottle—about 40 pills—and dumped them in the toilet.

I flushed.

"Drugs are eccentric" (Ronell, 1992: 29). I flushed, yes, but I went back like a married man to his mistress he vowed to stop seeing. Just as I was close to kicking this habit, to feeling like I could function without the Tramadol, on my next visit to Tijuana (three weeks after I flushed) I purchased a bottle of 50. I thought, why not. I thought, I could handle 50, take it easy, and that would be that. I liked the feeling, though, I liked how it kept me awake and I felt energetic (no physical pain) and could get a lot of writing done. I was more concerned with what was going on in my mind (research, theory, fiction) than what negative effects were happening in my body. "When the body seems destined to experimentation," Ronell (1992:7) contends,

> things are no longer interjected but trashed: dejected. The body proper regains its corruptible, organic status. Exposed to this mutability, the body cannot perverse its identity, but has a chance of seeing this fall, or ejection [...] When some bodies introduce drugs as a response to the call of addiction, every body is on the line [...] self-medication and vitamins become the occupations of every singularity.

Indeed, my own body had answered the call to addiction and I had no idea how I was going to get out the situation. For the time being, however, I did not care. I was an addict and I was okay with it—I had, as Karp (2006) notes some people do, entered into a committed relationship with the drug and was considering marriage. "Pill taking is a social act," Karp states (127). Ronell (1992:10) points out that "we do not know how to renounce anything, Freud once observed [...] The addict is a non-renouncer par excellence [...] however haunted or hounded, the addict nevertheless establishes a partial separation from in invading presence." So I did not renounce my use of Tramadol as I previously intended—I decided I would deal with it in the future. I was, in fact, terrified of facing the consequences of the withdrawal again—physically, emotionally, and mentally. If I did not take Tramadol at least every eight hours, of if I overslept, the pain would slowly creep through my body like a snake moving toward its prey, and I would start to feel depressed. In the previous withdrawal state, I felt overwhelmed by the outside world, by life; all I could think of were my past mistakes, my failures, and obsessed how I would fail again in the future. I thought of the people I hurt, and the people who had hurt me. I thought of love and how there was no love in my life at the moment and that maybe, probably, I would never experience love again. Basically, I was experiencing manic depression—it was a state I had never been in, *ever*, and I was not bi-polar. I have known bi-polar people and I could never understand how and why they could be happy and full of joy one day, and the next day change to bleak and suicidal.

I felt suicidal when I was withdrawing; I had even wrote suicidal emails to friends that caused many concerned phone calls. I sent an email to Liv, whom I missed very much, who had started me off on Vicodin, telling her I wanted to leave the copyrights to all my books and screenplays to her and her child, that I did not think I would be alive for very long.

Yes, that is how bad it was and that is why I was afraid of going off the drugs again. But why was I feeling the mania of outlandish depression, and why did a mere pain killing medication that was not narcotic-based make me feel energetic, sometimes elated, but okay with reality? Tramadol is not an SSRI like Prozac, Wellbutrin, Zoloft and many other anti-depressants; I learned it is an SNRI, which still affects seratonin levels of the brain that way an SSRI does.

Serotonin-norepinephrine reuptake inhibitors are a class
of antidepressants used for the treatment of depression
and other affective disorders. The drugs are sometimes

also used to treat anxiety disorders, attention deficit hyperactivity disorder (ADHD), obsessive-compulsive disorder (OCD) and chronic neuropathic pain. They act upon two neurotransmitters in the brain that are known to be essential to mood, namely serotonin and norepinephrine. This is in contrast to the more widely-implemented selective serotonin reuptake inhibitors (SSRIs), which affect only serotonin (Donaldson, 2006).

The reported side effects, reports Donaldson, from SNRIs "are dry mouth, nausea, and anorexia, drowsiness, dizziness, abnormal dreams, sweating, sexual dysfunction, insomnia, tremor, nervousness and hypertension." I experienced some of these—drowsiness now and then, dizziness if I took too much (as well as minor hallucinations), occasional sexual dysfunction (unable to reach orgasm, although I had no problems with erections), insomnia, and unusual dreams...I would not call them "abnormal" but curious. I had many dreams about writing. I would come up with ideas for fiction and essays. In one case, I dreamt about writing a book proposal; I woke up, wrote it, sent it out, and received a publication offer in two weeks. I seriously wondered if I would have came up with the idea for this book without Tramadol and the dream—in this case, did I owe the book do the drug, should I dedicate it to pills I was swallowing the way Burroughs owed heroin to many of his creative works, or Charles Bukowski owed to alcohol?

Karp (2006) owes his addiction for the gestation and publication of *Is it Me or My Meds?* The impetus for his inquiry was a desire to kick the habit of the pills he was hooked on—he had been suffering from depression all his life and could not sleep without a "cocktail" of doxepin, Klonopin, "and self-prescribed melatonin I had been taking every night" (p. 1). His attempt to free himself of the dependency was

> an awkward dance with medications. I discovered that stopping Klonopin was far more difficult than I had imagined. I had slowly tampered the dose over a period of three months [...] I made a full return to Klonopin; in fact, I now take twice the previous dose (p. 7).

I found myself in the same boat—returning to Tramadol, I was taking more than before. Now, I was up to fifteen-to-twenty pills a day, anywhere from six-to-eight at a time, depending how I felt and how long it would be before I took more (usually every seven hours works the best). Karp (2006) kicked the dozepin but not the Klonopin and decided that he was with the drug for life, married to it—his body and the medicine has entered a committed relationship. "Many people take for granted that addiction is a physical" (Dodes, 2002: 69). I have given consideration to the possibility that I may have a long-term (if not lifetime) agreement with Tramadol.[3] If so, I would have to continue to purchase it in Mexico (unless my finances improved)—the on-line price was triple what I paid for across the border and I imagined much more if I managed to get a prescription for a U.S. pharmacy.

Dodes (2002: 69) notes that the terminology "'hooked on' drugs [...] suggest that drugs somehow capture people." Am I prisoner to Tramadol and the way it makes me feel; am I trapped with the fear of how I will feel and react if I go cold turkey again? Karp (2006: 97) contends that with the contemporary fascination with the self and the search for who we are and the meaning of life, "drugs add another layer to search for self because they influence our feelings and moods." Already, Tramadol has influenced my writing and lead to publication; in that light, I do not see the harm, other than to my future physical self, which I am confident that I can deal with when the time comes. Karp (2006) points out the anthropology of pill-taking, that it is "social act"—if effects those around you as well as yourself, and the agency of addiction must consider the experiences of those who love and work with an addict. I have seen no negative affect on anyone in my life as a result of my addiction. I have arrived at a symbolic interaction the way Karp has, his "marriage to medication" akin to Blumer's (1969) theory of the "sensitizing concept." If marriage between two people is a "joint reality" (Karp, 2006:64) then the concept of being wedded to one's agreed addiction is to *accept* the reality that the drug creates *with* the addict.

Am I using academic jargon to justify being a junkie? Yes. In my fear of the reality without Tramadol, I have faced my fears by accommodating a socially unacceptable way of life. (Chopra, 1997: 4) writes that "fear of the past, fear of the future, fear of using the present moment for experiencing real joy—so many fears haunt the ways in which we have become immersed in addictive behaviors" is the unique condition addicts must deal with. Chopra views

the addict as seeker, albeit a misguided one. The addict is a person in quest of pleasure, perhaps even a kind of transcendent experience—and I want to emphasize that this kind of seeking is extremely positive. The addict is looking in the wrong places, but he is going after something very important, and we cannot afford to ignore the meaning of his search [...] the addict hopes to experience something wonderful, something that transcends an unsatisfactory or even an intolerable everyday reality. There is nothing to be ashamed of in this impulse. On the contrary, it provides a foundation for true hope and real transformation. (p. 4).

And that is how I see myself now—a seeker of truth, a body desiring transcendence and the truth. Every time I take the trolley down to the international border to get another bottle of my new reality, I am comfortable with the veracity I have embraced.

## Notes

1. I later learned that to get a prescription for almost anything, certain doctors would write one out for a fee of $25.
2. When I got hooked on Tramadol, each time I took the trolley down to Tijuana, I'd tell myself: "I just need the pain to go away, so I can get Project X or Project Y done, then I will cut back and quit." And: "Getting the project done is all that matters."
3. As I wrote this sentence, 9:30 a.m. on October 19, 2007, I ingested five capsules.

## References

Blumer, H. (1969). *Symbolic interactionism: perspective and method*. Englewood Cliffs, NJ: Prentice-Hall.

Burroughs, W. (1953). *Junkie*. NY: Ace Books.

Carrol, J. (1978). *The Basketball Diaries*. NY: Penguin.

Chopra, D. (1997). *Overcoming addictions*. NY: Harmony Books.

Denzin, N. *Interpretive interactionism*. (2001). Thousand Oaks, CA: Sage.

Domaldson, J. (2006). Serotonin-norepinephrine reuptake inhibitor information sheet. http://www.anxiety-and-depression-solutions.com.

Dodes, L. (1996). *The heart of addiction.* NY: HarperCollins.

Drugs.com. "Tramadol." http://www.drugs.com/tramadol.html.
Karp, D.A. (2006). *Is it me or my meds?* Cambridge, MA: Harvard University Press.

Labate A., Newton M., Vernon G., Berkovic S. "Tramadol and New-onset Seizures." *The Medical Journal of Australia* 182 (1), 2005: 42-43.

Ronell, A. (1992). *Crack Wars.* Lincoln, NE: University Nebraska Press.

# SPANKING THE DUNGEON GIRL

I knew Caroline from the blogosphere. I knew she was 29, lived in L.A., was into pain, worked as a submissive in a dungeon, and constantly craved a Jamba Juice®.

One time she wrote in her blog: *If anyone out there brings me a Jamba Juice to work, they'll get something special.*

I wrote: *If I lived in L.A., I'd bring you one every day.*

Her user handle was SoozyQ, Caroline was her pro name, and Elaine (apparently) her true name. She seemed obsessed with images of women in Nazi outfits and pictures of Edward Norton in *American History X*. For several months we exchanged blog posts about sex and drugs and loneliness. She kept late hours until sunrise like I did. One night she wrote she was upset because an ex-boyfriend had posted pictures of his dick entering her cunt on the Internet, and she gave me the link. She told me how she loved crystal meth because it made her horny and kept her thin, but she had to stay away from the addictive drug; I certainly could relate to that. She told me how the one night someone gave her what she thought was XTC but was actually acid and she had to work in that state of mind. I told her about the massive amount of shrooms I'd been taking lately and she said she didn't like shrooms "because they make me see witches." When asked what was the nicest gift anyone could give her, she replied: "A family and a home."

That was a good answer.

Ever since joining the blog universe, I've struck up about a dozen on-line "relationships" with women all over the country, from ages 18 to 48, varying in degrees of flirtatious emails, cybersex on Instant Messenger, late night phone calls when their husbands, boyfriends or parents are asleep, to some of them flying, driving or taking the Amtrak into San Diego for a weekend to see if there is any chemistry "in the meat world," as they say in the vernacular. Usually, it's awkward and doesn't work out...so with this, I often suggest, before they make the trip, that we immediately jump into a quick, hard fuck. Why not? That's why they're coming to see me, and sex will be on our minds the whole time—you know, who should make the first move, will a move be made, will there be sex, will the sex be good? If the sex is taken care of right away, then there won't be all that tension and anticipation and we'll both know if the sex is good and if we should continue with the visit as friends or mere tricks.

So I was a little nervous about meeting Caroline in L.A. and she said she was too, but I wondered about that since our pre-arranged get-together was going to be brief and contrived; she was a professional, after all, and I was going to pay her for the time at the going rate plus a tip; and I knew there wasn't going to be any actual "sex" involved.

This was also going to be a new experience for me, dropping into an S/M dungeon; I felt better that I was going to be with a woman whom I'd at least communicated with and knew a little bit about, rather than a complete stranger.

I've never been into the BDSM or D/s scene much; the "lifestyle" fascinates me and I like the clothing and gear and attitude in an academic sort of way, but it simply doesn't turn me on, nor is it something I pursue with the kind of passion that many in "the scene" do with almost religious fervor and intent.

I set up a Sunday appointment with Caroline at 1:30 p.m. The dungeon was located across the street from LAX in a warehouse zone on South La Cienega Boulevard. If you didn't have the address and didn't know what it was, you'd never know such a place of business was among the rows of bland, cookie-cut rectangular buildings that look like they were erected in the 1950s. The windows were tinted and there was an American flag in front of the place in question. I was told there was a "discreet" back entrance for clients who didn't want to be seen going in or out but I didn't care; I pressed the intercom and said I had an appointment and was buzzed inside.

The lobby was appropriately dark; a fat, greasy man in a pastel shirt who looked like the clichéd smut peddler sat behind a wooden desk. He looked me up and down and seemed bored. On a leather couch to my left was a woman with short hair, wearing a teddy and chewing gum; at the desk to my right sat a short blonde woman who was on a computer, doing something on the Internet—I knew this was Caroline; she was often on-line at work and I recognized her from some photos I'd seen: long, thick curly hair, round face, slightly chubby body, big breasts and innocent-appearing blue eyes.

I had two Jamba Juices® with me, orange and a berry flavor. She chose the orange and I had the berry.

She was shy and had a soft, high-pitched voice like a ten-year-old girl. She didn't look me in the eye when we shook hands, nor when she gave me a tour of the facility. But maybe this is what a submissive is supposed to act like, what did I know.

This dungeon was a 7,000 square foot warehouse split up into various themed rooms. The Bastille Room a jail cell with a rack; the Elizabethan Room a soft and pink and good for tickling; the "O" Room minimal with plain white walls and some hardcore torturing devices; the Mae West Room for clients who like to cross-dress and that door was closed; Windsor Hall was a classroom setting with half a dozen student chairs, a teacher's desk and a chalkboard; the Interrogation Room for some hardcore action and has quite the fascist feel; Windsor Stables was the "pony training" area and the biggest—it was like a studio sound stage or small theater.

"Movies could be made here," I said.

"Oh, there have been a few that have," Caroline said, looking at the floor.

"What kind?"

"What do you think?"

"S&M, I guess."

"And some porn."

I chose the Marquis de Sade Room, second biggest to Windsor Stables; everything in it was black or purple and there was a rack, cross, shackles, torture tower and a suspended cage connected to the ceiling and tracks, so it could be pushed from one side of the room to the other. I chose this room because it had a large, comfy couch with pillows. I would have wanted the classroom if Caroline had been wearing a schoolgirl outfit (she was in white lace) and I could be the perverted teacher and she the naughty nymph co-ed.

We went up front and told the fat man which room. "How long?" he asked me. I said half an hour and he said,

"$100." I already knew what the prices were going to be; an hour went for $160 and I almost took that but this was my first time, what if I got bored?

I gave the guy a $100 bill and Caroline took me to the equipment room, where I had the choice of dozens of whips, paddles, leather masks, and so on. I had no idea what to do so I went for the obvious: handcuffs. Then I grabbed some clothespins because I remembered a blog post of Caroline's about how she liked them clamped on her nipples. Then I randomly grabbed a paddle. "Ohhh," said Caroline, "that one's the worst. It's so hard."

It was a pretty heavy paddle and looked like it was made of walnut.

In the room, I said, "Okay, look, I told you I'm pretty cherry to all this so I have to say, I don't know what to do."

"Well, it's all about fantasy," Caroline said.

"But what are the dos and don'ts?"

"There's no nudity, you can't touch me on my private parts underneath my bra and panties, and there's no exchange of bodily fluids."

"Let's keep it simple," I said, "what if I gave you a spanking?"

"Okay. Where?"

"The couch."

I sat on the couch and she stood in front of me, looking quite demure.

"And I want you to call me Daddy the whole time," I told her.

"Daddy," she said, "lift up my skirt."

I did. She was wearing white thongs. She lay down across my lap. Her hair smelled like shampoo and I could also smell her pussy.

"Daddy, I've been so bad."

"Yes," I said, "you have," and I began to spank her, first on the left ass cheek and then on the right; back and forth like that, soft at first because I knew enough that you did this lightly and built your way up. Her ass was big and round and pink and her flesh jiggled.

I've had plenty of girlfriends who liked the occasional spanking—a smack on the rear while I fucked them in the ass or some playful stuff to get them excited, but I'd never done a "session" like this before.

As I spanked her harder, my hand began to hurt so I switched to the paddle. The hard wood against her butt made a reverberating sound in the de Sade Room. When I took my first hard swing, she tensed up and hissed and I saw that her ass cheek was bright red.

"I'm sorry," I said, "too hard?"

"Not at all, Daddy."

"Harder?"

"If you wish, Daddy. Hurt me good, Daddy."

So I did...and I got into it. It took me maybe fifteen minutes to get into what this was all about, and when I did, I loved it. Her butt was turning black and blue and she was crying out and squealing and sometimes her body went completely stiff and she'd shudder. But in my mind, she was no longer a woman I knew from the Internet whom I was paying to do this to; she was Tara, my ex-girlfriend who had walked out of my life four months ago, who'd abandoned me and our cats and left me with the full rent and utilities to pay, who'd left me alone and never wanted to see or talk to me—yes, she was Tara and I was punishing Caroline (Tara) for what Tara had done, for hurting me: I was hurting her back. "You bitch," I said (in my mind, not out loud) as I slammed the paddle down, "you cunt, you piece of worthless shit," and I guess I got too carried away because Caroline said, "Okay, okay, that's too hard, not that hard, Daddy."

Her ass was completely red with several black and blue spots. Her body was shaking and covered in sweat. I was hot and sweating too. I felt bad that maybe I'd gone too far, so I rubbed her back and stroked her hair and ran my fingers up and down her legs; my hand moved between her legs, keeping above the thong panties, and she was wet—I could feel it, see it and smell it. She was enjoying this, I guess. She said, "Give me some more, Daddy."

So I did, but not too hard and I couldn't get back into the fantasy that I was punishing Tara; I pretended I was her evil Daddy and she was my daughter and she was a bad girl and I was going to have incest with her all night long. I told her this and she said, "Oh yes Daddy I want you to fuck me tonight, I want my Daddy's dick inside me because I'm such a *bad little slut.*"

"You are bad," I said and began to use the paddle harder to keep my mind off the hard-on I had that was pressing against her stomach and that she knew was there because she began to grind her torso into my crotch.

The buzzer went off, our half an hour was up. I could have gone for another thirty minutes but this was good enough. Caroline stood up; her make-up was smeared and there were tears down her bright pink face.

"Okay?" I asked.

She smiled. "I would've been more verbal but I was just trying to survive that paddle. Oh man," and she lifted her skirt and looked at her backside in the mirror on the wall, "my ass is gonna to be a mess tomorrow."

I got up and we both grabbed some cheap motel style towels to wipe off sweat and tears. We stopped and looked at each other and then hugged.

I gave her a $50 bill as a tip, hoping it was a good tip.

I then gave her a kiss and she closed her eyes and smiled.

"Thanks for the new experience," I said.

"Come back again when you're in L.A."

"I will."

"Maybe get a second girl, double your fun."

The other girl was asleep on the couch in the lobby. The fat man nodded at me. I walked out of the dungeon like I was being released from county jail and the sun was very bright. I didn't feel dirty like I thought I would. I felt—fuck if I know—cleansed in a way. It was an auto/ethnographic moment: epiphany, reflection, emotional sociology all rolled into one.

I felt less angry.

I may have even been a little happy.*

---

* I was worried I'd crossed the line with her, that I damaged her flesh beyond $100 and a $50 tip. I emailed her about it and she replied: *Not at all. If you had gone too far I would have TOLD YOU. Oh, my ass is really black and blue, YOU. It's beyond my skin and muscle, it's a bruise right down to the bone. It hurts to sit. That's so COOL-IO!*

# INTERPRETATIVE INTERACTION
# IN LA LA LAND

## NOTES ON CHASING THE DREAM
## TO CREATE VISUAL CULTURE

There is an abundance of myth and misrepresentation about life in L.A., and what it takes to get a movie made. As Denzin (1989: 11) notes:

> American cinema has been constantly pulled by the competing tendencies to present the horrible...inside a melodramatic structure which represses while it valorizes and contains...the unpresentable within a narrative format that resolves itself either through a happy ending, or through ambiguous closures which permit viewers to complete the story to their own satisfaction. A level of reflexivity exists within these narratives, which informs the viewer that this is a story, after all, and it may not be real life, and if it is like real life, what is seen here doesn't happen to everybody.

A certain "notorious" actor we'll call V.G. is on the phone and he wants me to read passages of my script to him.

"—that one part, when he turns into the demon, read it again, man, but *slower.*"

He's on his cell phone, driving toward Malibu, or out of Malibu—I only know he's stuck in traffic on PCH.

116

"*Slow*er," he says, "I wanna absorb the meaning of every syllable," instructing me like he we're having sex.

I imagine him talking that way to women when they give him blowjobs, which he apparently gets a lot of. A couple of years ago he put out a "controversial" indie film that had an actual blowjob scene, no tricks, between him and a certain well-known actress. The bj was the talk of Cannes, mid-America, the subject of billboard ads. In La La Land, it was an advertising trick to be laughed at—but one that work. People talked about the movie a lot; they didn't watch it, or like it when they watched it, but they *talked* about it. Lately, V.G. has been running around the clubs and bars of La La Land and finding young women—the starfuckers—to re-enact that scene from his movie. He has set up a website for women to blog on their experience—did they like it, did they love his cock, the taste of his semen, were they grossed out, were they drunk, did they regret it, would they do it again, was it just like in the movie, and so on. The blog is an interesting space for these women to bash him, bash each other, and engage in flame wars, all over his now-famous penis.

Now, I am reading him sections from my screenplay, *End of the Line*, on the phone from my beach apartment in San Diego while he is stuck in traffic getting in or out of Malibu. He is deciding if he wants to attach to the project. Thing is, he does not read scripts, even when filming. He refuses to read or memorize. He prefers the screenwriters to read to him.

I wouldn't mind having him attached to the project; I wouldn't mind seeing this script made into a film—it's why I wrote the goddamn thing.

*End of the Line* is a slasher-exploitation-dark comedy about a crime documentary crew that decides to commit their own grisly, absurd homicides to have better stories to cover. Along the way, they film a re-enactment of a botched demon-raising ceremony that ends in mass murder; the actors re-enact the ceremony correctly and summon forth a demon who takes over the body of the one of an African-American characters who has a '70s-style blacksploitation afro. Best line: *"Holy shit — the nigger is a demon!"*

The script came out of a story idea that Brandon Riker and I had. Brandon is an old friend who has been living on the fringes of La La Land business, managing the giant Regent Showcase Theater in West Hollywood, hanging out with the B-list crowd, roommates with an ex-girlfriend of Q.T.'s. The roommate said if we came up with a good idea for a horror movie, she could set up a meeting for us to pitch it to Q.T. and maybe he'll executive produce it.

The first ten pages come from notes given to us by Q.T. How that happened is like this –

Kelly Greene and I had driven up from San Diego for two meetings with La La Land producers. This was back when she had the idea of chasing the dream of contributing to visual culture. She was an actress but knew she was too old to start from square one and compete with women ten years younger and weren't afraid to move to La La Land to chase the dream. She decided she'd write screenplays with me, the apparent professional writer, and enter the business that route.

One meeting was about our romantic comedy with a wedding motif. The other was with a former exec at Universal who had helmed such timeless classics as *Beethoven* (the dog movie) and *Shakespeare in Love*. The meeting was part of the prize package for my winning best screenplay in one of those many screenplay contests. It was called *Stations*. We had gone to a film festival the month before when it was a finalist for an award judged by John Milius—*that* excited me because Milius had written such timeless classics as *Apocalypse Now* and *Red Dawn*. We went to a party attended by such timeless cultural luminaries like Gary Sinese, Patricia Heaton, and Ken Starr—yes, *that* Ken Starr.

We seemed to be on a path to La La Land, or so we thought.

The meeting with the ex-exec from Universal took place at a coffee shop in Westwood. His advice was to find a rich person in San Diego who wanted to produce movies and get them to fund *Stations;* or find an unknown actress who knew a rich person that wanted to jumpstart her career (a.k.a. a sugar daddy). "That's how indie movies are made today," he said; "you don't have to live here in La La Land, you can make indies anywhere, in your backyard, and get them seen."

I was starting to come to terms with the fact that my little drama would never be purchased or produced by a studio or big production company, no matter how many people loved the writing and the story. It simply was not commercial.

Kelly and I drank coffee at the Starbucks on Santa Monica and Wilshire, looking at Creative Artists Agency across the street, at all the nicely dressed people going inside and out. Young agents in black suits sat around us at Starbucks. If I was smart, I would start a conversation with one; I had scripts in my briefcase and Liv had a dozen headshots in a manila folder. I'm not that smart, or bold.

"Over there," I said to Kelly, nodding at the CAA building, "American cinematic history is being made as we speak; deals are sealed, ideas are pitched, careers are planned."

She had no idea what I was talking about; she had no idea how important, how much power, CAA had in this town—she was probably the only actress in southern California who didn't. It was then I knew why she would never become the screen actress she always dreamt of.

The second meeting was in the bar of the Peninsula Hotel. The Governor was lunching there; Highway Patrol officers working as security surrounded the hotel. We were meeting with a supposed producer of a supposed hot little company. She gave us notes. She was well-dressed and funny. Later, I would learn she was a con artist acting like a player, one of the dozens I would meet in La La Land as I continued to market my work.

Kelly was not paying attention to the meeting, though; she was preoccupied comparing herself to all the other women there—the way they dressed, walked, how much selective surgery they had.

"I will never be able to compete," she said; "not with all this *plastic.*"

"Is that why everyone is so bright and shiny?"

In the bar, two young girls, age 10, were sitting in a corner, in private school uniforms, their own credit cards, eating lunch.

"They are so prim and proper," Kelly said; "their parents are probably wheeling and dealing in the dining room. Why can't life be like *that* for *my* daughter?"

She wanted to get out of the Peninsula fast. She felt uncomfortable. She realized, for the first time, that she was a stranger in a strange land, she did not belong here after all, she would never live this kind of life, the life she once dreamt of.

That was why she did not stay to meet Q.T. The meeting wasn't for sure—a big maybe. At first she was going to stick around and see if it happened; she was a fan of his movies and wanted to meet him, dreaming of his discovering and casting her. Now, she wanted to high-tail it out of La La Land after experiencing real life at the Peninsula.     She     dropped me off at the Regent Showcase where Brandon was still at work. She used the bathroom there. We both tried to talk her into staying.

"But it's not for sure," she said.

"It's 50/50," Brandon said.

"I should just go home," she said.

She was acting like she was mad at me. She didn't even hug me goodbye. She got into her SUV and sped off to the 101 and back home.

"There she goes," I said to Brandon, "always running away."

"She'll regret it, if the meeting goes down."

"Yeah, well, *will* it?"

He shrugged.

I crashed on his couch, in his apartment near the Farmer's Market in the Fairfax neighborhood. It did not seem like good things would happen. His roommate was nowhere to be found. We got drunk; I fell asleep.

I woke up to the sound of loud laughter. I opened my eyes and a certain well-known B-movie actor, we'll call him M.M., was looking down at me like he often in his movies.

"It's alive," this actor said.

Q.T. was there, surrounded by Brandon's roommate and five scantily-clad models/actresses (I would later find out they were paid call girls) who kept asking for more crystal meth. The apartment was too small for all these people and there was not enough booze. Q.T. wanted to go back to his place; he said he had a still in the backyard, and more meth and cocaine. The five girls liked that idea.

We drove up into the Hollywood Hills, partied at Q.T.'s house. We drank his homemade moonshine and snorted cocaine. I didn't want any meth. I don't even like coke, but how could I pass up the opportunity to snort it with Q.T.? I thought: *No one in San Diego will ever believe this, especially Liv.* In La La Land, people would say, "Who *hasn't* done blow with Q.T.?" More people joined the party, mostly hangers-on and wannabes, whores and players.

In his screening room, Q.T. showed us his first black and white short film, shot on 16 mm. It was then that Brandon and I pitched him the idea of *End of the Line.*

He seemed to like it—enough to jump in and offer suggestions as to how the opening should be shot. All our mouths were moving fast in a cocaine frenzy of cinema language. It opens with a stand-up comedy routine by a Hassidic Jew, with hair locks and a yarmulke and the whole black and white outfit—a stand-up comic by night who had a day job working for a crime documentary crew.

That is the part V.G. might play if he attaches.

V.G. is uncertain about his ability to interpret a character that is a comedian. He is uncertain about comic timing. Actual stand-up is not his thing, black comedy and weirdness is.

So he is having me read the stand-up routines in the script, having me do it the way a comic would.

He calls me five times a day for two weeks, still unable to decide if he wants in on the project. A good friend of his may direct it, option it. The option is contingent to V.G. getting on board.

(Brandon had given the script to a horror actress/model, who was sleeping with this producer/director, who is friends with V.G.)

"Fuck these phone calls," he finally says; "get your ass up here and let's do this shit face-to-face."

That sounds like a good idea. I'm getting sick of waiting for this screenplay to be optioned and maybe made.

"You should be in La La Land anyway," says V.G., "if you wanna make it in this biz."

It's what I have been telling Kelly for months.

Instead of talking about the script, or me reading it to him, V.G. and I spend most of our time together at bars and looking at, talking to, women. Everywhere we go, he gets attention and the women flock to him. I don't get any attention. I don't like this. V.G. is short, scrawny, unbathed, and obnoxious. He insults the women we meet; half of them giggle and take it and the other half tell him to fuck off and walk away. Still, he is a movie star, or some kind of star, and the starfuckers make their play to add another to their notch. They don't notice me until he introduces me. Who am I? I'm just some writer. I don't even live here. *What have you done? How do you know V.G.? Well, since you know V.G., I'll blow you too.*

"You owe me," V.G. says as we drive down Sunset Boulevard; "how much pussy have you gotten because of me?"

"They're all dirty skanks," I say. "I mean, really…"

"There *are* stupid," he says, laughing, "but that's La La for ya. Ain't gonna find any chick with brains here, not like the East Coast. Back East, women can think and put two comprehendible sentences together. You owe me, Hemmingson. Set me up on a date with a San Diego chick."

The only person I can think of is Jolene, who is getting ready to leave her boyfriend and move to La La Land and chase the culture-making dream. She is interested in meeting La La men, especially those connected. I show V.G. her website with photos.

"Nice," he says. "Does she put out?  Is her cunt tight or loose?"

"I don't know."

"You don't *know?* You haven't *done* her?"

"She's just a friend."

He can't understand this—women are to fuck and suck with, not be friends with.

"Give me her number," he says, "I'll talk to her."

When I tell Jolene I gave him her cell phone number, she freaks out. She thinks he is a disgusting human being and has no interest in dating him. "But you've never met him," I say and she says, "I've heard stories," and she says, "I've seen his pictures---*eww.* This better be a joke, you asshole," she goes, "you better *not* have given my number out to a guy like that."

Half of me wants V.G. to call her, just to see what happens, because I bet she'd go out with him just so she can tell people she did; the other half of me hopes he doesn't call her, because she'll probably be mad at me.

It's very loud in the Viper Room. V.G. can't stand the women trying to talk to him. They don't seem to like him either, but they stand next to him anyway in case there are paparazzi around. He wants me to come outside and discuss something. He seems mad at me.

Everyone is pissed off at me these days. Liv doesn't speak to me anymore; doesn't answer emails or phone messages.

V.G. has an issue about a party we were both at last week. I went there with Dominique, who I based the female lead of *End of the Line* on. I introduced her to the woman who had passed *End of the Line* on to that producer/director who might option it. She and Dominique hit it off. They were "hot for each other," as they say, especially after a few drinks. They wanted to leave and have fun. The three of us went back to my room at the Motel 6 on Hollywood and Whitley.

"You vanished," he says; "I heard things."

"What things?"

"Did you have a threesome with...?"

I smile.

He is infuriated. How come he wasn't invited? After all he'd done for me, he was left out—how could I do such a thing?

I don't tell him that both the women didn't want him to be there; I had suggested it. "He's gross," Dominique said. "I've already had him," the other woman said, "and it's all hype."

"How could you bail on me like that, man," he says. "That just doesn't *happen*. I mean, who the hell *are* you, man? You're *nobody*. You're just some fucking *writer*."

"And you're the movie star who always gets what he wants," I say. "Did your giant ego get bruised?"

V.G. drops his drink and takes a swing and hits me in the jaw. I didn't see that one coming. People outside the Viper gasp, go quiet, look at us.

I hit him back, in the mouth. His lip bleeds and my knuckles are in pain.

He hits me again.

I hit him back—again.

He tackles me, pushing my body against the wall.

I hit him in the side several times and we call each other bad names.

Three bouncers split us apart.

"That's enough," they say.

V.G. and I are both out of breath, bleeding, and in pain.

"I'm sorry, man," he says; "that was rude."

"Ouch," I say.

"I'm really sorry," he says.

Maybe I had it coming, but I won't admit this out loud.

"I'll buy you a couple of drinks," he says, "c'mon."

We are allowed back in to the club, but told we'll be banned for life if we start it up again. At the bar, V.G. and I have a couple of tall vodka tonics and laugh about it all, telling people what just happened outside and isn't it too bad TMZ.com wasn't there...

It's the last I ever see or talk to him.

The script doesn't get optioned.

# HERE COME THE NAVEL-GAZERS

## DEFINITIONS AND DEFENSES FOR AUTO/ETHNOGRAPHY

## INTRODUCTION

My approach to "what is auto/ethnography" (herein "a/e")[1] is from the perspective of a subaltern pedagog.[2] I present my answers to that question while following the definitions of Ellis, Bochner, Denzin, Reed-Donahay, et al., cited in the previous essays, who have practiced and pontificated on what is (and is not) a/e for many years and in many publications. One should not, however, accept that their definitions are sacrosanct and without a place for change. A/e is an evolving form, malleable in its shape, approach, and use. Think of a/e as a big piece of silly putty, and today is the time to play.

This final essay for this book presents several definitions from primary source scholars and subaltern voices; a number of critical points ("navel-gazing") that question a/e as a valid method of qualitative inquiry; the responses/defenses to these critiques; my own definitions; a 15-point plan that addresses the changing nature of a/e in the 21st Century; and my theory (and contention) that we have now entered the Eighth Moment of qualitative research.

# DEFINITIONS

Holt (2003) explains a/e as

> a genre of writing and research that connects the personal
> to the cultural, placing the self within a social context
> (Reed-Danahay, 1997). These texts are usually written in
> the first person and feature dialogue, emotion, and self-
> consciousness as relational and institutional stories af-
> fected by history, social structure, and culture (Ellis & Bo-
> chner, 2000). Reed-Danahay explained that autoethnogra-
> phers may vary in their emphasis on *graphy* (i.e., the re-
> search process), *ethnos* (i.e., culture), or *auto* (i.e., self).
> Whatever the specific focus, authors use their own experi-
> ences in a culture reflexively to look more deeply at self-
> other interactions. By writing themselves into their own
> work as major characters, autoethnographers have chal-
> lenged accepted views about silent authorship, where the
> researcher's voice is not included in the presentation of
> findings.

Beverley (2000) views a/e is a form of "testimonio" for the
subaltern to have a voice. "The *testimonio* is a first-person political text told by a narrator who is the protagonist or witness
to the events that are reported on" (Lincoln & Denzin (2003:
18). Furthermore:

> Finding a space for the subaltern voice suggests a new lo-
> cation for voice, that is, in personal narratives, autobiog-
> raphies, and autoethnographic texts. In autoethnography,
> researchers conduct and write ethnographies of their own
> experience. If we study our own experiences, then the re-
> searcher becomes both the research subject and its object
> [...] A variety of terms and methodological strategies are
> associated with the meanings and uses of autoethno-
> graphies, including personal narratives, narratives of the
> self, writing stories, self stories, , auto-observation, per-

sonal ethnography, literary tales, critical autobiography, radical empiricism, evocative narratives, reflexive ethnography, biographical method, co-constructive narrative, indigenous anthropology, anthropological poetics, and performance ethnography. The autoethnography can be read as a variation of the testimonio, or the first-person life history (p. 19).

Ellis (2005: xix) defines a/e as

research, writing, story, and method that connect the autobiographical and personal to the cultural, social, and political. Autoethnographic forms feature concrete action, emotion, embodiment, self-consciousness, and introspection portrayed in dialogue, scenes, characterization, and plot. Thus, autoethnography claims the conventions of literary writing.

Basically, a/e is a fusion of personalized social science and methods used in the humanistic forms of the essay, poetry, and fiction; it is "the postmodern successor of both ethnography and life history" (Bloor & Wood, 2006). Social movement writers now engage "their own experiences as participants to understand social movements" (Ellis, 2002: 402). In a peer review of a book manuscript of mine (Hemmingson, 2008), a reviewer/reader presented an explanation of a/e that I feel is succinct and on the mark:

[It is] an emergent method in a new postmodern ethnography known by varied terms not altogether indicative of similar meanings or methods but rather more the outcome of change and transformative approaches to other qualitative methodologies such as reflexive and literary ethnographies that shift the focus of participant observation to the "co-observation of participation." When the procedure

129

features the personal lives of the author framed by a cultural context the methodology is increasingly being referred to as "autoethnography." Influenced by a postmodern challenge to the representation of a cohesive view of the world and conceptualizations of universal truths this approach favors a constructionist epistemological perspective making both a methodological and theoretical deployment of performance-driven strategies as the researcher becomes the subject of study for data collection, representation, and the interpretation of embodied and intersubjective knowledge. This lends a highly introspective and personal orientation to autoethnography that reveals multiple aspects of consciousness and self-consciousness that are personally and/or politically emancipatory. Not surprisingly, autoethnography interrogates issues of power and authority across the entire spectrum of the research process including the conceptualization of the research project, its implementation, and textual production. Leading practitioner, Carolyn S. Ellis, often frames her discussions of autoethnographic ontological and epistemological concerns in ethical and redemptive terms as a means to subjective and intersubjective knowledge about life and circumstances in a cultural context. For her, autoethnography is an "ethical practice" that makes use of morality and reason to overcome adversity, which presents one with difficult choices requiring communication with the other. Thus, the autoethnographer insider introspectively monitors, recalls, and examines in profound detail "physical feelings, thoughts, and emotions." These are chronicled in the first-person voice and are used to reveal and understand the relational and socio-cultural self through narrativity including short stories, essays, poetry, journal entries, etc. Autoethnographers warn the method is not meant to be used by anyone, and will not work if the author/subject lacks the talent to write evocatively.[3]

Crawford (1996: 158) argues that "taking the ethnographic turn, living and writing the ethnographic life, is essentially a self-report of personal experiences [...] the ethnographer is unavoidably in the ethnography one way or another, however subtly or obviously" and notes

> I must include some account of myself [...] the reflexive turn of fieldwork for human study by (re)positioning the researcher as an object of inquiry [...] An unstable/ subjective self, the reduction of distinctions, the surfing of perspectives, the high-speed juxtaposition of the private and global, and the like may be features of autoethnographic account [...] a kind of guerilla action and subversive discourse that productively challenges and changes the traditional and, in my judgment, transparently flawed ways of experiencing, portraying and acknowledging ethnography (pp. 167-9).

There is another school of definition, however. Pratt (1992) defines a/e as the way a secondary ("colonized") culture present themselves in same way their dominants have represented them. For Pratt, a/e is not the exploration of the self in culture, but a collaboration of mixed ideas and values forming both the dominant and submissive cultures. That is, one culture presents itself to ethnographers the way a second culture views them—for survival purposes, integration. When one culture subjectively sees another via their own bias and desires, the culture gazed on starts to change and adapt to the perceptions of the gazer. This is group a/e of a single culture or society, unlike the a/e that is about a single person within a culture, or the lone ethnographer's life studying the Other in a foreign culture. "A good interpretation of anything [...] takes us into the heart of that which it is the interpretation" (Geertz, 1973: 18). Pratt's definition is political and falls

131

under the rubric of postcolonialism; in her theory of a/e, the colonizers written and oral misrepresentations change the colonized. This definition, however, can be integrated with other definitions of a/e and can be a response to how the Other gazes on the auto/ethnographer. For instance, Lee (2008) addresses this issue as a Chinese-Canadian woman reflecting on her experiences of anti-Chinese racism in Canada; people who do not know her or her history make assumptions, tell her to "go back to China" although she is a Canadian native. She is seen as a foreigner in a nation originally made of colonists. She writes, "After many years, so much education, I suffocate by the ignorant rantings of a deranged local resident" (1). Lee's a/e approach shows two perspectives on one culture's reality: hers, and the Other; she reveals and examines the Other's viewpoint, and presents to readers how she prefers to be perceived by the outside world, or what her "truth" is. The Other wants to impose its perception on her and she refuses to adapt to that interpretation. Lee's work is an example of what Clough (2006: 280) calls "the most developed form of experimental ethnographic writing."

## ANTI-REFLEXIVITY:
## CRITIQUE OF THE NAVEL-GAZERS

"It is generally not wise to conduct a study of the 'self'" Holt (2003: 7) is advised by peer reviewers of one of his a/e papers. Obviously, not everyone in the social sciences is keen on the a/e method. Ellis (1995) recounts the resistance of peer reviewers when she was exploring the form in the early 1990s, told that the self was not a sufficient sample for scientific study. Detractors contend a/e lacks a cosmology within the global complexities of human sciences, and is limited in scope as a "self-anthropology" (Strathern, 1978). Some critics believe "stories" are not scientific research (Holt, 2000); that personal experience is self-indulgent and narcissistic (Mikhaylowskij, 1995: 230-232, Sparkes, 2002: 211) and the auto/biography is extravagant and confessional, not true research methodology (Goodall, Jr. 2000). The anti-reflexivity camp ask why would any responsible body engage in self-indulgent navel-gazing when a/e is difficult to validate and present as rigorous or replicable (Holt, 2003). A/e is "irreverent, self absorbed, sentimental and romantic" (Ellis & Bochner, 2000: 736), "a movement away from trying to understand the world of the 'other'" and "a turn away from praxis" (Ellis, 2002: 400). Gannon (2006: 491) refers to a/e as "the (im)possibilities of writing the self" and notes "it is clear that just 'being there' is insufficient as any guarantee of truth." Jacobsen (1991: 122) states: "The experience of the ethnographer into an account does not necessarily shed light into the account of others." Some condemn a/e to be "without guidance, experience and patience this process can, for many, result in nothing more than pointless self-absorbing introspective 'navel gazing' excessive subjectivity and self-delusion" (Boufoy-Bastick, 2004: 10) and that "the force of the ontological is impoverished" (Probyn, 1993:) when the self takes over. There is an attitude in some circles that a/e is not a contribution to knowledge—this is only true because it is not *allowed* to be knowledge and not *allowed* to be research at institutions that have imposed restrictions, censorship, and "rules of method." But who is "not allowing" this, who is saying, "You cannot do that, you have to do it this way"? There were once similar viewpoints regarding the television replacing the radio, video replacing film, digital replacing the analogue, the computer replacing the typewriter, the scroll replacing the codex and movable type replacing the scroll.

## DEFENSES FOR NAVEL-GAZING

I suggest there is a "culture war" against a/e, and the division has much to do with class and generation, similar to past opposition of the poststructuralist, Marxist, and postcolonial theories and methods in various disciplines. (Some things take time.) These are the scholars who do not want to see change and fear evolution within the comforts of their so-called rigid disciplines and grounded theories; these are the "professors" who claim to be the expert and adopt the familiar "my way or the highway" attitude when it comes to method, form, and representation of research and critical thinking. We can construct knowledge about ourselves and textualize that knowledge and that process seems to scare certain "academics." Poulos (2008) comes to the defense of a/e by pointing out that

> the "self-indulgent navel-gazing" charge is a straw man argument, combined with a simple ad hominem attack. It is usually intended to belittle and bully. As such, it may carry emotional weight, but it has no merit. It is a bit like the U.S. conservatives of the Rush Limbaugh/Anne Coulter stripe who throw the word "liberal" around as though it were unequivocally and naturally a pejorative term. Of course, as I glance back at my 50 years on this planet, I can honestly say that I have met very few "self-indulgent navel-gazers" (most people, in my experience are, in fact, less than satisfied with their navels), and most of them were people who either smoked too much high-octane weed or who suffered from narcissistic personality disorder. The prognosis was not good, and none of them were

writers. If, by this charge, the critics mean that introspection or reflection are bad per se, I have nothing to say other than "Try it sometime." But I think what most of them are saying is that we should not "indulge" our emotional lives because emotions can lead us astray. Indeed, they can. On the other hand, most of the great literature, art, music, writing, poetry, etc. in the history of humanity has tapped into the great and deep energy of pathos to move the human soul to new highs and lows.[4]

"I know no better response to the charge of navel gazing than to quote a friend of mine, Ron Pelias, who says that 'the navel tells the story of our first connection to another'"(Ellis, 2008).[5] Burnhard (2007: 809) argues that a/e "must be more than navel gazing or self-disclosing for its own sake." "While able to slip into the worst sort of navel-gazing, the best examples of auto-ethnography draw [on] self-awareness, empathy and reflexivity" (Galloway 2007). Along with empathy, a/e must be honest and just; in order to be so, a/e will have to reject those who wish to impose restraints and censorship that keeps it away from honesty and fairness. The self-anthropologist should not take offense to the label "navel grazer" and should see the truth in those words, embrace the concept. It is the navel that first gave us life, where we once breathed while in the womb, connecting us to our closest Other (as Ellis notes Pelias), our mother (of course, for some, this may be a negative relationship) via the umbilicus. I urge narcissistic researchers to desire a closer relationship with their navel, *and to interview their navel*, which would be akin to the self-interview, or auto-interrogation. I would also suggest asking questions of the umbilical chord. That may sound absurd but you must know I am speaking symbolically; the umbilical chord, lost to us since the day of our birth, is something that must be re-found, re-discovered, re-connected to. Here is an example: today, as I write this (February 25, 2008), I had to pay a visit to my mother and get a copy of my birth certificate. I looked at the old document, processed on a manual typewriter in 1966, and I felt disconnected from my "self," that body of the newborn. I asked, "Is this me?" This piece of paper represented an infant fresh to the world, his navel deprived of the umbilicus it had known for months, in comfort. Here this piece of paper said my mother was sixteen-years-old and my father eighteen. They were children themselves, they were hippies, they were people I never knew and to this day do not understand. My mother's listed address is in a neighborhood I would never set foot in today; it is a gang territory. I was amazed how baffled I felt, how much of my identity vanished from me as I gazed on this slip of government documentation. I knew I had to become an ontological detective and find my lost umbilical chord, and speak to it, understand it, query it, which would result in a re-understanding of my self.[6]

## MY TAKE[7]

"In using oneself as an ethnographic exemplar," Gergen and Gergen (2002: 12) contend,

> the researcher is freed from traditional conventions in writing. One's unique voicing—complete with colloquialisms, reverberations from multiple relationships, and emotional expressiveness—is honored. In this way the reader gains a sense of the writer as a full human being.

The anthropological enterprise has always been concerned with how people experience themselves, their lives, and their culture (Bruner, 1986). A/e "reverses the traditional epistemology of qualitative methods found in the naturalist approach" (Bloor and Fiona, 2006: 19). In light of this, I present a 15-point plan[8] (or manifesto) on what a/e could be, could strive for, and how petitioners of the a/e method can approach and conduct their self-research in the 21st Century:

1. A/e should be naked and honest, no matter how painful that may be. We experience enough censorship in our every day lives from our immediate culture: family, employers, institutions of higher learning, and the government; so we should not engage in self-censorship. Being honest could result in not being published or approved; or could cause one to be shunned, ostracized, censured, condemned, and put in general "hot water." The self-inquiry then is this: how much do I value the truth and my integrity?

2. A/e should seek to create its own form of "standard presentation" and reject the requirements of institution, unless of course one is seeking publication in a journal that strictly adheres to one format, such as the usual introduction-literature review-method-findings-conclusion. We have already seen many unique and individual approaches in a/e representations, often referred to as "experimental." There needs to be more of this. Nothing is set in stone.

3. A/e should embrace the navel and the gaze upon it with relish.

4. A/e should seek the umbilical chord—that is, the origination of the gaze.

5. A/e should reject the views and reviews of committees. Since a/e is about the personal and the individual, no committee can ever truly understand such

things. The plural does not feel comfortable among the solo.

6. A/e should at all times question anyone who professes to be an "expert," even if such expertise is canonized in publication and cited often by others. Since a/e is about the personal, the *definition* of the form is also personal (just as the personal is political and has different meanings for every individual). In this case, then, a/e makes use of symbolic interactionsim; the method of writing and the definition of category may have a certain meaning for one person that does have the same meaning for another.

7. A/e should never *compromise* but always be willing to *embrace* change and new definitions.

8. A/e needs only one sample: the self.

9. A/e is an argument *for* reality, not *of* reality.[9]

10. A/e is an agreement with memory.

11. A/e is arrangement of personal truth.

12. A/e is a champion for universal truth.

13. A/e should seek to amend and redeem the self's trespasses and wrongs of yesteryear, employ a way of positive change in the now, and offer hope (through reflection) for tomorrow.

14. A/e should strive to be a torch song of the soul (Jones, 2003), not a textbook for the academy.

15. A/e now belongs in the eighth moment in the social sciences.

## THE EIGHTH MOMENT –
## ANOTHER MODEST PROPOSAL

*The seventh moment has passed, and the eighth is now here.*

"The seventh moment is concerned with moral discourse, with the development of sacred textualities" and "asks that the social sciences and humanities become sites for critical conversation about democracy, race, gender, class, nation-states, globalization, freedom, and community" (Denzin & Lincoln 2000:3). Denzin & Lincoln (1994, 2000, 2003) have postulated a theory of "the seven moments in qualitative research." The theory is fairly well-cited now and I will be brief—the first moment was the "traditional" period (early 1900s); researchers aspired to "objective" accounts of field experiences, concerned only with the other and rigorous science. The second moment was the so-called "modernist" era (post-WW II through the 1970s), where we found qualitative research striving to be as meticulous as its quantitative equivalent. [10] The third moment (1970-1986) was the "blurring of genres." The fourth (mid-1980s) is the "crises of representation" where the "trying knots in the handkerchief" (Lincoln & Denzin, 2003) of qualitative inquiry occurred and the started to become accepted and legitimized in the halls of academy. The fifth moment defines the marriage of "experimental writing and participatory research."

The sixth is the "postexperimental" and the seventh is where fictional ethnographies (Frank, 2000), ethnographic poetry (Richardson, 1999; Royce, 2002) and performance ethnography (Denzin, 2003) are welcome. The sixth and seventh moments came about in 1999-2000 and went into full swing after September 11, 2001. What the seventh moment did not, at that time, take into account was the increased rate of speed in technology (Virillo, 1983) and on the Internet, and how these devices can be used for qualitative inquiry—particularly a/e—in what is now the *eighth moment.* Furthermore, the eighth moment is defined as an era of *complete rejection* of all previous rules, theories, and restrictions, where the preceding "experts" step aside and make room for the new (although not necessarily "younger") voices. The age of the subaltern is here. "We will maintain our power and influence to the extent that we can do this, that is to make the world bend to our vision" (Denzin, 2007: 1, quoting Sullivan, 2007: 84).[11]

A/e is no longer limited to the written word. Martineau (2001: 242) studies the sculptures of Bill Reid as works of a/e that "became powerful interventions in Haida and Canadian politics and cultures, and helped initiate changes in the ways relations between the cultures are negotiated and understood." A/e is now being used as a method in film and video (Russell & Russell, 1999), documentaries, music, podcasting, and video blogging, or the vlog. A/e mixes fiction with real accounts (Frank, 2000, 2002) although what is taken for autobiography has always been considered as form of fiction anyway (Denzin, 1989)—memory is selective and the auto/biographer is biased in the telling of "true" events. This is no longer an issue in the eighth moment, where we will find (and do find) a/e being practiced on MySpace.com, livejournal.com, Facebook.com, and YouTube; that is, digital ethnography. For instance, we now see people using the vlog to engage in lifewriting, or *lifevlogging* and *ethnoblogging*. The vlog is personal, political, global, universal; it transcends race, class, even gender.[13] What the vlog does is put the gazer face-to-face to the visual and verbal auto/biographer, and this, I contend, is the future of a/e and all matters of research into the self: a continued process of the cultural turn (Jameson, 1998) that is always re-defining rather than becoming inert.

Another emerging method of a/e is the reality show. Think of this—in some reality shows, the subject, whose life is being broadcast on television, can replay events and choices on the screen, reflect on these televised moments of their lives, and debate how things would have been altered if they had made a different choice. For example, in dating shows and a show like *Cheaters*, where people catch their spouses or companions with another lover, the subjects often reflect on how they felt when first learning the truth of the two-timing other or being "eliminidated" or rejected; they verbalize what they think of the shattered relationship or date. Their reality is vicariously experienced and changes before our eyes. Contestants will maintain blogs and vlogs during and after the show, and continue to look back on their experience, whether it was a good or bad time, and how it changed them. In some cases, the rejection of a date, lover, or spouse is traumatic; on TV, they feel the pain of failure, the loss of possibilities Reflection and analysis of one's life is a tenet of a/e; in this case, "reality" shows will indeed operate as a new form of a/e in the eighth moment. "Reality shows" will no longer be restricted to broadcast television by networks; the vlog is a reality show, the podcast is a reality show, performance ethnography is a "reality" show.

## CONCLUSION

At the top of this essay, I said a/e is malleable. I am not the only subaltern voice to suggest that the seventh moment has come and gone and new approaches and perspectives are called for—de Beer (2003) makes an effort to "discuss 'a seventh moment bricoleurship' and 'narrative turn to poetics' and explain how it evolved."

> The development and active experimentation with art and poetry in research took off in the sixth phase or *post-experimental* moment (since 1995). Data poetry as a meth-

odology or technique, and as alternative and complementary form in presenting different voices and data is thus officially recognized within this framework and I will present various examples. As these 'moments' are not like geological seams that are mined to extinction, but overlap and are often working simultaneously, I particularly advocate the *seventh moment* (since 2000) of appreciation and recognition of various methods and perspectives of qualitative research. Though, I also dispute that, within my current context and experience, research has not yet come close to the sevenths moment and that the positivist research paradigm is still very much favoured particularly within certain geographical and institutional power-knowledge-discourse confinements. I argue that poetically represented data has a valid place in the development and strengthening of qualitative research and that it has a resonate methodology and theoretical base. It strengthens personal reflective narrative writing, promotes an epistemology for consciousness.[10]

de Beer's definition of the seventh moment is "when researchers cease debating differences and celebrate the marvelous variety of their creations." The new data poetry in the eighth moment is technology with speedy change, and how technology can be adapted—and adopted—for qualitative research. The fact is, a/e is not as "new" as it may seem to some who have recently been indoctrinated. The meta-fictionists and deconstructionists in the humanities were using a/e methods in the late mid-to-late 1970s and throughout the 1980s in fiction, poetry, and the literary essay, breaking down the wall between "author" and "character" and turning narrative constructs inside-out with reflection and subjectivity. Today, this is no longer the "experimental" and is considered ineffective and trite (McCaffery, 1993). Federman (1994) and Mann (1999) have both declared that postmodernism faded away, even died, around the time reflexive ethnographers were *starting* to embrace it. McCaffery (1986) contends post-modernism was born the day John F. Kennedy was assassinated, whereas the postmodern turn, or the fifth moment as explained by Denzin & Lincoln, did not occur until the late 1980s. "I am writing today about the End of Postmodernism [...] I am in the process of burying Postmodernism" (Federman, 1994: 107), in which case, current postmodernism is a zombie. Mann (1995) determines that most postmodernist discourse and schools of thought today are part of the "stupid underground" (p. 127) and merely methods of vain masochism, or "masocriticism." Mann states "it would be excellent if the farce [...] could be brought to an end" (p. 19).

If the postmodern is indeed dead, and such labeled discourse is futile and an act of self-inflicted cruelty, where does this leave the navel-gazers and their narcissistic methods? *The answer: within the aesthetics of the eighth moment.* It has been acknowledged that Western science has its shortcomings (Herman, 1996). So how does a/e catch up with the times and other disciplines (it seems literature and film are now entering the ninth moment)? *The answer: by the speed of technology and the subaltern voices moving to the forefront.* For a/e to grow, thrive, and come into its own within the eighth moment, the colonizers (the former leading experts) have to vacate the continent and stop telling the colonized, "This is right and this is wrong." In the eighth moment, as far as a/e is concerned, there is no longer a correct or an incorrect method, *only the method that works best for the individual auto/ethnographer.* It is time for the "professors" and "teachers" of the fifth, sixth, and seventh moments to step down from the lectern and discontinue imposing dusty limitations. What is the best methodological approach to lifewriting, the personal essay, au-

143

to/ethnography, the blog, the vlog, reality television, podcasting, theater, and any other form of navel gazing? The answer: whatever works best for the voice shouting of its life (the performance) in the flesh or cyberspace, embracing the navel, aware of the umbilicus, experiencing the freedom of expression within the confines of an imposed "discipline." Even Denzin (1994: 307) said, "We must invent a new language, a new form of writing that goes beyond autoethnography [...] This must be a language of a new sensibility, a new reflexivity, refusing old categories," in which case, one hopes that he, being one of the colonists, will indeed banish the old categories and rules, move aside, and open the roadway for the subaltern to drive and thrive.

## Notes

1. The spelling varies from autoethnography, auto-ethnography, and auto/ethnography the same way auto/biography is. I prefer using the latter of the three, also used by Reed-Danahay (1997).

2. "Subaltern" commonly refers to the perspective of persons from regions and groups outside of the hegemonic power structure, often used in postcolonial theoretical writings. Some thinkers use it in a general sense to refer to marginalized groups and the lower classes—a person rendered without agency by her or his social status (Young, 2003). Gayatri Chakravorty Spivak uses it in a more specific sense, arguing that subaltern isn't

> just a classy word for oppressed, for Other, for somebody who's not getting a piece of the pie [...] In postcolonial terms, everything that has limited or no access to the cultural imperialism is subaltern—a space of difference. Now who would say that's just the oppressed? The working class is oppressed. It's not subaltern....Many people want to claim subalternity. They are the least interesting and the most dangerous. I mean, just by being a discriminated-against minority on the university cam-

pus, they don't need the word 'subaltern' [...]They're within the hegemonic discourse wanting a piece of the pie and not being allowed, so let them speak, use the hegemonic discourse. They should not call themselves subaltern (de Kock, 2003).

This essay adheres to Spivak's advice. I am using the discourse to engage in my "piece of the pie" in what a/e is and is not.

3. I gratefully acknowledge the reviewer, whoever they are.
4. Taken from Poulus' posted response on the critics of a/e at groups.yahoo.com/autoethnograhy.
5. Quoted from the same thread at the Yahoo Group.
6. I also seek to interview other people's umbilical chords and navels not as a researcher of a/e, but as a *traditional ethnographer*. There is a whole new set of cultural samples here (the umbilicus of the Other, the subaltern navel) that has yet to be explored, and is the topic of a different essay.
7. "Everyone is entitled to their *informed* opinion." – Harland Ellison.
8. This is a modest proposal. I am not on a soapbox and professing to be the expert...yet.
9. Denzin (1989) cites Elbaz (1987, p. 1): "autobiography is fiction and fiction is autobiography: both are narrative arrangements of reality."
10. During this moment, C. Wright Mills (1959) published his influential treatise, *The Sociological Imagination* that provided a blueprint for all the other moments.
11. Of course, Denzin is one of experts and colonizers who have imposed rules and methods that I am calling for Eighth Moment auto/ethnographers to reject and rebel against.
12. de Beer presented her paper at the British Educational Research Association Annual Student Conference, Heriot-Watt University, Edinburgh, 10 September 2003.
13. The Internet erases gender, glass, and race. Baudrillard (1993: 56) says "the TV watches us." Now, literally, with web cams, the Internet watches us as watch it. But we can never be certain that the image we are seeing is true, just as the watcher cannot be certain we are true. But that does not matter. In the eight moment, the

truth only matters to the auto/ethnographer engaging his and her truth.

# References

Baudrillard, J. (1983). *Simulations*. NY: Semiotext(e).

Baudrillard, J. (1987). *The ecstasy of communication*. NY: Semiotext(e).

Beverley, J. (2000). Testimonio, subalternity, and narrative authority. In Norman K. Denzin and Yvonna S. Lincoln, eds. *Handbook of Qualitative Research* (2nd Edition, pp. 55-65). Thousand Oaks, CA: Sage.

Blumer, H. (1969). *Symbolic interactionism: perspective and method*. Englewood Cliffs, NJ: Prentice-Hall.

Bloor, Michael and Fiona Wood. (2006). *Keywords in Qualitative Methods: A Vocabulary of Research*. Thousand Oaks: Sage.

Boufoy-Bastick, Béatrice (2004). Auto-Interviewing, Auto-Ethnography and Critical Incident Methodology for Eliciting a Self-Conceptualised Worldview. *Forum: Qualitative Social Research* 5(1). Retrieved February 15, 2008]. at: http://www.qualitative-research.net/fqstexte/1-04/104boufoy-e.htm

Brumann, Christoph (1999). Writing for culture: Why a successful concept should not be discarded. *Current Anthropology, Supplement 40*, S1-S27.

Bruner, E.M. (1986) Experience and its expressions. In Turner, V.W. & Bruner, E.M. *The anthropology of experience*. Urbana: U. of Illinois P.

Bruni, Nina (2002). The crisis of visibility: Ethical dilemmas in autoethnographic research. *Association of Qualitative Research, 2*(1), 24-33.

Burnard, P. (2007) Seeing the psychiatrist: an autoethnographic account. *Journal of Psychiatric and Mental Health Nursing* 14 (8), 808–813.

Clough, P. T. (1997). Autotelecommunication and autoethnography: A reading of Carolyn Ellis's "Final negotiations." *The Sociological Quarterly,* 38(1), 95-111.

Clough, P.T. (2006). Comments on setting criteria for experimental writing. *Qualitative Inquiry,* 6(2), 278-291.

Crawford, Lyall. (1996) Personal ethnography. *Communication Monographs.* 63, 58-170.

de Beer, M. A seventh moment bricoleurship and narrative turn to poetics in educational research. Available at http://www.leeds.ac.uk/educol/documents/00003137.htm

Denzin, N.K. (1994). Evaluating qualitative research in the poststructural moment: the lessons James Joyce teaches us. *Qualitative studies in education,* 7, pp. 295-308.

Denzin, N.K. (1989). *Interpretive biography.* Newbury Park: Sage.

Denzin, N.K. (2001). *Interpretive interactionism.* Thousand Oaks: Sage.

Denzin, N. K. and Lincoln, Y. (eds.) (2000). *Handbook of qualitative research* (2nd Ed). London: Sage.

Denzin, N.K. and Lincoln, Y. (eds.) (2003). *Collecting and interpreting qualitative materials.* Thousand Oaks, CA: Sage.

Denzin, N.K. (2003). *Performance ethnography: critical pedagogy and the politics of culture.* Thousand Oaks: Sage.

Denzin, N.K. (2007) From the president. *International association of qualitative inquiry,* 3 (4) 1, 10.

de Kock, L. (1992). "Interview With Gayatri Chakravorty Spivak: New Nation Writers Conference in South Africa." *A Review of International English Literature,* 23, 29-47.

Ellis, C. (1997). Evocative autoethnography: Writing emotionally about our lives. In W. Tierney& Y. S. Lincoln (Eds.), *Representation and the text* (pp. 115-139). NY: SUNY Press.

Ellis, C. (1995). *Final negotiations.* Philadelphia: Temple UP.

Ellis, C. (2002). Being real: moving inward toward social change. *Qualitative studies in education,* 13 (3), 399-406.

Ellis, C. (2004). *The Ethnographic I: A Methodological Novel about Autoethnography.* Walnut Creek: AltaMira Press.

Federman, R. (1994) *Critifictions.* Albany: SUNY Press.

Frank, K. (2000). "The management of hunger": using fiction in writing anthropology. *Qualitative inquiry,* vol. 6, no. 4, pp.474-488.

Frank, K. (2002). *G-strings and sympathy.* Durham: Duke UP.

Galloway, A. "Where's Chris? (on reflexive design)." Retrieved February 25, 2008 at http://www.purselipsquarejaw.org/2004/10/wheres-chris-on-reflexive-design.php

Gannon, S. (2006). The (im)possibilities of writing the self-writing: French poststructural theory and autoethnography. *Cultural Studies ↔ Critical Methodologies,* 6 (4), 2006 474- 495.

Geertz, C. (1973). *The interpretation of culture.* New York: Basic Books.

Gergen, M.M. & Gergen, K.J. (2002). Ethnographic representation as relationship. In Bochner, A.P. & Ellis, C., eds. *Ethnographically speaking: autoethnography, literature, and aesthetics.* Walnut Creek: AltaMira.

Goodall, Jr. (2000). *Writing the new ethnography.* Walnut Creek: AltaMira Press.

Goode, E. 2006. Mixing genres: it¹s floor wax and a whipped topping! *Symbolic interaction,* 29 (2), 259-263.

Harman, W. W. (1996). The shortcomings of Western science. *Qualitative inquiry* 2(1), 30-38.

Hemmingson, M. (2008). *Zona Note: An Auto/Ethnography of Desire and Addiction.* Newscastle-on-Tyne, UK: Cambridge Scholars.

Holt, N. L. (2001). Beyond technical reflection: Demonstrating the modification of teaching behaviors using three levels of reflection. *Avante,* 7(2), 66-76.

Holt, N.L. (2003) Representation, legitimation and autoethnography: an autoethnographic writing story. *International Journal of Qualitative Methods,* 7(1), 1-22.

Jameson, F. (1998). *The cultural turn.* London: Verso.

Lee, K.V. (2008). White whispers. *Qualitative Inquiry* (in press).

Lincoln, Y.S. and Denzin, N.K. (2003) *Turning points in qualitative research: tying knots in a handkerchief.* Walnut Creek: AtlaMira Press.

Lionnet, F. (1990). Autoethnography: the an-archic style of dust tracks on a road." In *Reading Black, Reading Feminist.* Henry Louis Gates, Jr. (ed.) NY: Meridian, 382-414.

McCaffery, L. (1986). *Postmodern Fiction: A Bio-Bibliographical Guide.* New York & London: Greenwood Press.

McCaffery, L. (1993). *Avant-Pop: Fiction for a daydream nation.* Boulder: Black Ice Books.

Mann, P. (1995). *Masocriticism.* Albany: SUNY Press.

Martineau, J. (2001). Autoethnography and material culture: the case of Bill Reid. *Biography,* 24 (1), 242-258.

Mills, C. W. (1959). *The sociological imagination.* NY: Oxford UP.

Mykhalovskiy, E. (1996). Reconsidering table talk: Critical thoughts on the relationship between sociology, autobiography, and self-indulgence. *Qualitative Sociology,* 19, 131-151.

Poulos, C. (2008). "Critics of autoethnography." Post at groups.yahoo.com/autoethnography. http://groups.yahoo.com/group/autoethnography/message/1613

Pratt, M.L. (1992) *Imperial eyes: studies in travel writing and transculturalism.* NY: Routledge.

Probyn, E. (1993). *Sexing the self: Gendered positions in cultural studies.* London: Routledge.

Reed-Danahay, D. (1997). *Auto/Ethnography: Rewriting the self and the social.* Oxford: Berg.

Richardson, M. (1999). The anthro in cali. *Qualitative Inquiry,* 3(4), 363-365.

Riessman, C. K. (1993). *Narrative analysis.* Newbury Park: Sage.

Royce, A.P. (2002). Shaman. *Qualitative Inquiry,* 8(2), 284.

Russell, C and Russell, R. (1999). *Experimental ethnography: the work of film in the age of video.* Durham: Duke UP.

Sarbin, Theodore R. (1986). The narrative as a root metaphor for psychology. In Theodore R. Sarbin (Ed.), *Narrative Psychology: The Storied Nature of Human Conduct* (pp.3-21). NY: Praeger.

Shoemaker, Sydney (1963). *Self-Knowledge and Self-Identity.* Ithaca: Cornell UP.

Siegesmund, Richard (1999). Reflecting on the I in inquiry. *Getting Good at Qualitative Research Symposium* presented at the Annual Meeting of the AERA, Montreal Canada, April 19, 1999.

Sparkes, A. C. (2000). Autoethnography and narratives of self: Reflections on criteria in action. *Sociology of Sport Journal, 17*, 21-41.

Sparkes, A. C. (2002). Autoethnography: Self-indulgence or something more? In A. Bochner & C. Ellis (Eds.), *Ethnographically speaking: Autoethnography, literature, and aesthetics*. Walnut Creek: AltaMira.

Strathern, M. (1987). The limits of auto-anthropology. In Anthony Jackson (Ed.) *Anthropology at home. ASA Monographs, 25,* pp.16-37. London: Tavistock Publications.

Trinh, T.M. (1991) *When the moon waxes red*. London: Routledge.

Turner, V.W. & Bruner, E.M. (1986). *The anthropology of experience*. Urbana: U. of Illinois P.

Young, Robert J. C. (2003). *Postcolonialism: A very short introduction*. New York: Oxford University Press.

Every human being is a universal singular.

--Norman K. Denzin, *Interpretative Interactionism*

# About the Author

Michael Hemmingson is a novelist, filmmaker, playwright, journalist, and ethnographer; needless to say, he writes in many genres about many subjects. His other auto/ethnographic book, *Zona Norte*, is about two years of research into sex and politics and the self in Tijuana, Mexico. He is a staff writer for the *San Diego Reader* and a two-time holder of the Helm Fellowship at Indiana University's Lilly Library. Other academic books include *The Dirty Realism Duo: Charles Bukowski and Raymond Carver on the Aesthetics of the Ugly, Gordon Lish and His Influence on Twentieth Century American Literature: Life and Times of Captain Fiction, The Reflexive Gaze of Critifiction: Studies in Contemporary American Metatext, The Anthropology of Pornography: An Ethnographic Account of Los Angeles Sex Workers, Raymond Carver: An Interpretive Biography, Women in the Work and Life of Raymond Carver, William T. Vollmann: Freedom, Redemption, and Prostitution, William T. Vollmann: An Annotated Bio-Bibliography*, and *Star Trek – TV Milestone*. His first feature film, *The Watermelon*, was produced by LightSong Films in 2008.

Lightning Source UK Ltd.
Milton Keynes UK
UKOW05f2208120717
305218UK00001B/96/P